**FRANCIS OF ASSISI
AND HIS WORLD**

San Diego Christian College
2100 Greenfield Drive
El Cajon, CA 92019

271.3092
F815A
G168f

Francis of Assisi and His World

Mark Galli

Downers Grove, Illinois

To Barbara, who exhibits many of Francis's finer qualities

Francis's first celebration of the nativity was much more primitive than this rendition. *The Christmas Celebration at Greccio* by Giotto di Bondone.

Previous pages: The lifelong mysticism of Francis is portrayed in the *Ecstasy of St Francis* by Giotto di Bondone.

Page one: Francis, painted 36 years after his death. *St Francis* (c. 1262) by Maestro di San Francesco, from a series of panels from San Francesco al Prato, Perugia.

InterVarsity Press
P.O. Box 1400, Downers Grove, IL 60515-1426
World Wide Web: www.ivpress.com
E-mail: mail@ivpress.com

©2002 Mark Galli

This edition copyright ©2002 Lion Publishing

Published in the United States of America by InterVarsity Press, Downers Grove, Illinois, with permission from Lion Publishing.

All rights reserved. No part of this book may be reproduced in any form without written permission from InterVarsity Press.

ISBN 0-8308-2354-9

Printed and bound in China

Library of Congress Cataloging-in-Publication Data has been requested.

P 15 14 13 12 11 10 9 8 7 6 5 4 3 2 1

Y 08 07 06 05 04 03 02

Contents

Introduction

Francis, especially
during his
conversion, often
walked the fields
below Assisi.

E veryone loves Francis. His statue (usually with a bird on his arm) is found in gardens all across the world. His example is touted as much needed in our day. Francis, the patron saint of ecology. Francis, the peacemaker. Unfortunately, in our attempt to make Francis relevant, the man we have come to love resembles only a distant relative of the real Francis.

Francis was less interested in ecology and peacemaking than we are. And when he did focus on these themes, he did so for unmodern reasons. His were medieval reasons. This can be a problem for modern people. If someone today wants to condemn an idea or practice, few one-liners do a better job than, 'That's so medieval.' Everyone nods and chuckles. No one has to say what everyone thinks: 'Indeed. How irrelevant.' What is surprising, though, is that, in Francis's case, it is those medieval reasons that make him both relevant and vital for our day.

This book, then, is an attempt to understand the

modern medieval Francis. First, it tells the story of Francis. It does not try to tell the reader what scholars think of other scholarly opinions of Francis. Nor does it weigh scholarly arguments about the facts of Francis's life. The careful reader will see that a great deal of scholarship has been consulted in writing the book (see Suggestions for Further Reading, page 184). But scholarship has been used to enable the author to tell Francis's story concisely, and to tell it in an engaging way.

Too many biographies of Francis get bogged down in scholarly debate. Others tell his story without any historical distance, so that Francis comes across as someone who walked about a foot above the ground. Here, I attempt to keep the narrative moving while employing (usually behind the scenes) the best scholarship available to help bring detail and life to the story.

Second, the book is about Francis's world. It is not a social history. It will, hopefully, pique the reader's curiosity to explore the medieval world even more. Here, the reader will get only a glimpse of life in the Middle Ages – but enough of a glimpse to set Francis's feet firmly in his world.

As the book progresses, then, the reader should gain a deeper understanding of who Francis really was, and why he taught and acted as he did – as a medieval man living in a medieval world. It is only then that readers will see his real relevance to modern world. And, just in case I have not been clear enough in the narrative, I have outlined my conclusions in chapter 13.

As I have noted, many books have helped me to navigate Francis and his world. The most helpful have been Omer Englebert's classic *St Francis of Assisi: A Biography*, and the more recent *Francis of Assisi: A Revolutionary Life* by Adrian House. Anyone familiar with these books will see my debt to these fine scholars.

Nearly all of the quotes from Francis or his early biographies come from the two volumes (soon to be three) of translated Francis documents: *Francis of Assisi: Early Documents*, edited by Regis J. Armstrong, J.A. Wayne

Hellmann, and William J. Short. The work of these and other scholars was a continual source of awe and thanksgiving for me. Their patient labours on matters of the closest detail freed me to concentrate on simply telling Francis's story in an economical and, I trust, engaging way.

My editors at Lion, Morag Reeve and Jenni Dutton, have never ceased encouraging me and have shown great forbearance as I missed not one, but two deadlines. Every writer should be blessed with such editors.

Finally: for the past year, my wife, Barbara, my daughters, Katie and Theresa, and my son, Luke, have not had as much access to me as they wished sometimes. But their patience and understanding have made it possible to produce a better book, if not a better husband and father.

Europe at the time of Francis

Smolensk

POLAND

RUSSIAN PRINCIPALITIES

Kiev

Vienna

HUNGARY

SERBIA

BULGARIA

KINGDOM OF SICILY

EPIRUS

LATIN EMPIRE

Constantinople

NICEA

SELJUK SULTANATE OF ICONIUM

ARMENIA

CRETE

CYPRUS

Antioch

AYYUBID SULTANATE

Acre

Jerusalem

The Knight

It was a brisk November day in 1202 when Assisi's militia marched through the city's streets. Citizens cheered as troops filed out of the city gates, down to the expansive plain that spread out below the city. Meanwhile, the militia of rival Perugia across the plain was also on the march, and by mid-morning the two armies studied each other tensely from less than a kilometre away.

Then Perugia charged. Suddenly the plain was filled with the thunder of hooves and the shouts of men intoxicated with fear and hate and the sheer joy of battle. For the next few hours, the fighting raged over the plain, spilling into the woods and private castles. Sweat and blood poured from man and beast, as merchants, farmers and nobility – called upon to defend their rights and to uphold their town's honour – swore and slashed at one another and then ran, some in pursuit, others for their lives. One contemporary historian noted, 'The final defeat came very late, but the slaughter was very severe.'

Assisi's army was defeated and then slaughtered. Those who tried to hide in the thick woods or in caves were hunted down like animals. Some were taken prisoner; others were mercilessly killed.

One chronicler, in overblown rhetoric that nonetheless captures the victors' pride, said that one river was so swollen by the blood of the dead that its banks overflowed. An Assisian partisan wrote, 'Oh, how disfigured are the bodies on the field of battle, and how mutilated and broken are their members! The hand is not to be found with the foot, nor the entrails joined to the chest; on the forehead horrible windows open out instead of eyes… Oh, you of Assisi, what a sad day and what a dark hour was this!'

It was an especially dark hour for Assisi's elite

Opposite page:
Armies clash in a medieval battle scene attributed to Niccolo da Bologna.

company, Compagnia dei Cavaliera, and particularly for one 21-year-old member of that company, a wealthy merchant's son. Like all young men of his day, he had spent much of his youth memorizing the songs of the troubadours – ballads of knights and ladies, and the glory of battle. Now he found himself bound in chains, dragged off as a prisoner across a battlefield littered with the bodies of childhood friends, through Perugia's streets, which were lined with taunting onlookers. Though the young man remained remarkably upbeat during the first few weeks of his imprisonment, he had already begun saying goodbye to the happy and heroic dreams of his youth.

New politics

The prisoner's Christian name, given by his mother at his baptism in autumn 1181, was John. The name did not please his father, Peter Bernadone. He had been away, again, on business to France when his wife, Pica, gave birth. When he returned, he insisted on calling the boy Francis. The name stuck.

Peter Bernadone was the type of husband and father who was used to having his own way at home. Increasingly, he was the type of citizen who also had his own way in his home town. This was partly due to his ambition, and partly due to changes in the social and political climate.

When Peter first started out in business, he and his fellow merchants complained much about their lack of voice in civil government. They complained about the crushing by taxes and forced labour imposed on them by the *majores* – the noblemen, knights and lords who gained their ranks and property by accident of birth. In fact, for as long as he or anyone could remember, in Assisi (and, for that matter, in all of Italy, France, Germany and Britain), *minores* such as Peter had been subject to the *majores*. To be sure, with the accident of birth came the responsibility to protect those lower on the social scale from robbery, rape, pillaging by foreign armies and so on. But the price the *minores* (made up of serfs and villeins) paid for this protection became increasingly oppressive. The serfs had essentially become slaves, belonging to the lord's land like so much livestock, enjoying no independence. Villeins – farm labourers, craftsmen and merchants such as Peter – were free in theory and had the right to own property. But between the taxes and forced labour, their freedom was difficult to enjoy.

However, things had begun to change in Peter's grandfather's day. Even Peter's father would have recalled that, in his day, the only markets available to craftsmen and labourers were the local castle, monastery or town. But the Crusades opened up new trade routes. It was not long before ships crammed Mediterranean harbours, and caravans travelled along rebuilt Roman highways (destroyed centuries earlier by invading barbarian armies). Raw materials and manufactured goods found their way from one end of Europe to the other. The upshot was that many artisans and merchants reaped fortunes. Among

You are where you live

Writers enjoy waxing eloquent when describing the region in which Francis lived, for the area is believed not only to have inspired Francis's love of nature, but also to have had something to do with shaping his paradoxical character. A typical example comes from the pen of historian Omer Englebert:

Umbria, where St Francis's life was spent, is situated in Central Italy, between the Marches of Ancona and Tuscany. This region, full of contrasts and beauty, affords to man's spirit a variety of scenery which is truly captivating: solitary peaks and charming valleys, streams lazily meandering along the plain, torrents cascading down ravines, fields of wheat and unproductive volcanic soils, forests of ilex and fir, silver-leaved olive trees, engarlanded vines running along the mulberry trees, and clumps of black cypress mounting guard at wayside chapels. The winter is rugged, the summer scorching, autumn and springtime marvellously mild.

these fortunate merchants was Peter Bernadone, who made his money in cloth.

By the time Francis was born, visitors to Assisi had told how in some towns, the authorities – both the nobility and the church – were granting economic privileges to wealthier merchants. They were even admitting them to their councils. Merchants in many Italian towns helped to choose public officials, made and administered law, and meted out justice. These new political arrangements were called 'communes', and the commune's 'citizens' (those who owned a home and earned sufficient income) were now bound to a new 'lord' – the community – obliged by a feudal oath to,

Sir Geoffrey Luttrell and two ladies are the very image of medieval chivalry. English manuscript illumination (c. 1340).

among other duties, place themselves as troops in the commune's service.

Francis, boy romantic

The rising Peter made sure that Francis and his only brother, Angelo, got at least a minimal education. He sent them to the school at San Giorgio Church in Assisi. But Francis was never much of a student; he barely learned to read and write, and always preferred to be read to. He wrote even less. As an adult, he was considered 'a man without learning', meaning that he never undertook advanced studies in theology or law.

It was not the life of the mind that captured the boy's imagination, but the cult of chivalry, then all the rage. In his youth, Francis sat rapt at the tales of travelling French troubadours. They sang at civic gatherings and tournaments, extolling the legends of Charlemagne and the Knights of the Round Table, celebrating love and women. He heard stories of love purified by sacrifice and loyalty; of devout knights who, 'without fear and without reproach', served in the holy crusades; of

Charlemagne,
one of the
most celebrated
kings of the
Middle Ages.
Fifteenth-century
Viennese
manuscript
illumination.

repentant warriors who, in atonement for their sins, built churches to the glory of God.

In addition to his impatience with learning and his romantic imagination, Francis was barely supervised by his parents. They pretty much let the boy do as he pleased. Bonaventure, a later biographer, put it discreetly in his *Major Legend of St Francis* (1260–63), saying that Francis 'lived among foolish mortals and was brought up in foolish ways'.

In short, Francis was spoiled. He was allowed to shirk his studies and pursue a carefree life. He was especially fond of whiling away the hours with friends: 'He was so accustomed to setting his heart on joining his companions when they called him,' writes the author of *The Legend of the Three Companions*, an early biography, 'he would leave the [family] table even if he had eaten only a little.'

Like many middle-class boys, Francis and his friends mingled with the sons of nobles (this mixing of social classes was another sign of the changing times). They partied together. They danced through the streets, serenaded young ladies late into the night (sometimes being rewarded for their singing by the more willing ladies). They also committed their share of juvenile vandalism and thievery.

Francis, it seems, was born for this lifestyle: 'He was an object of admiration to all, and he endeavoured to surpass others in flamboyant display of vain accomplishments,' writes Thomas of Celano in *The Life of St Francis* (1228–29). He was known for his 'wit, curiosity, practical jokes and foolish talk, songs, and soft and flowing garments'.

He was a natural leader, and many young men were anxious to be in Francis's presence, especially if it meant flirting with the law and social custom. 'Thus with his crowded procession of misfits, he used to strut about impressively and in high spirits,' making his way through the streets of Assisi at all hours of the day and night, as

Celano records. It felt especially cruel, then, when the witty, amiable, carefree Francis found himself languishing in a Perugia prison for a year.

Assisi becomes a commune

That this happy son of Assisi found himself imprisoned was due both to parochial rivalry and international politics. The news was full of war and rumours of war. If some powerful lord blocked a road and demanded a toll, or if a rival commune claimed rights to a coveted forest, the threatened city sent in troops to settle the issue. This sometimes meant besieging a castle, razing a town, burning crops or taking and torturing prisoners.

Pope Innocent III (who reigned in 1198–1216), hardly a paragon of virtue in such matters, nonetheless was alarmed at those who 'continue to lay waste cities, destroy castles,

'That man, whom today we venerate as a saint... miserably wasted and squandered his time almost up to his 25th year of his life.'

THOMAS OF CELANO, *THE LIFE OF ST FRANCIS*, 1228–29

The medieval meal

As in our day, most medieval people wanted meat with every major meal. However, most people had to settle for it only on special occasions. Francis's family, wealthier than most, probably could afford meat more often. Beef, pork, chicken, squirrel, porpoise, magpie and peacock were all typical. A variety of spices and sauces were used to flavour food. One English recipe for broth instructed the cook to boil diced rabbit with almond milk, cypress root, ginger, rice flour and sugar.

Poorer families ate peas and beans, but the wealthy often tried to avoid vegetables, except for onions. Fresh fruit would have been available, certainly in Italy, and the most common were apples and cherries. Wine was the choice of the rich, and ale the choice of the poor. The poorest of all had to be satisfied with water.

Most families had to cook for themselves, but it is likely that Francis's family had a cook to bake bread (again, the rich would be more likely to have an oven), prepare meals and set the table.

*'In the time of
St Francis, the
people laughed
at the agonies of
enemies who
were tortured
and killed...
They shed blood
now in arrogant
wholesale
slaughter, now
with delicacy.
Revenge – the
vendetta –
became a fixed
idea.'*

ARNALDO FORTINI,
FRANCIS OF ASSISI,
1992

burn villages, oppress the poor, persecute churches, and reduce men to serfdom. Murder, violence, and rapine are rife, with quarrelling and wars'.

It was not just local flare-ups that were problematic. All through Francis's childhood, Assisi had been in a state of near constant civil war with the Holy Roman Emperor. Assisi merchants had rebelled against imperial control less than a decade before Francis's birth, in 1174, only to be crushed within three years by Emperor Frederick Barbarossa. Frederick installed a trusted lieutenant, Conrad, Duke of Spoleto, in La Rocca castle overlooking Assisi, and this kept the town in check – at least until 1197.

That was the year in which the next emperor, Henry IV, died. With no clear successor in view, German politics was thrown into chaos. It was a signal for a general uprising throughout Italy. Communes drove out imperial representatives and occupied imperial fortresses. The newly elected (in 1198) Pope Innocent III, seeing an opportunity to enlarge the church's power, supported the rebellious cities. He ordered Duke Conrad to hand over Assisi, and the duke, judging his situation hopeless, capitulated. He left La Rocca castle in the care of a German garrison, and headed for Narni to do homage to papal legates.

As soon as Conrad was out of sight, Assisi's militia besieged the castle. Assisi resented imperial control, to be sure, but they were in no mood to merely switch masters. Papal legates pleaded with them to back down. Assisi refused. They then threatened Assisi with excommunication – again, to no avail. The Assisi militia, of which Francis was likely a part, took the citadel by storm and dismantled it, stone by stone.

This was the occasion when Assisi organized itself as a commune. The first order of business was to provide the city with a secure perimeter. The men of the city, probably including Francis, threw together a rampart, using stones from the dismantled fortress as material.

Then the commune began the reprisals. Many outlying

castles still pledged themselves to the emperor, and continued to levy road and bridge tolls. A resentful Assisi militia attacked and destroyed castle after castle. They also ransacked the Assisi homes where the nobility lived for part of the year. Some of the elite of Assisi's aristocracy, including the family of six-year-old Clare di Favarone (the future St Clare of Assisi), fled to Perugia, and pledged themselves and their lands to their new protector. Perugia, naturally, was only too happy to welcome them.

While Assisi was busy destroying castles, Perugia launched a series of raids across the Tiber (Tevere), the river which split the plain between the two cities, and began harassing Assisian landowners. Matters escalated when Perugia made an alliance with Foligno, 19 kilometres from Assisi. Assisi, in turn, made treaties with Gubbio, Fabriano, Nocera, Spello and Narni – all towns which had scores to settle with Perugia.

A 12th-century French troubadour, who represents a way of life that inspired the young Francis.

When, in November 1202, Assisi launched a pre-emptive attack, Perugia was amply prepared. The only Assisians not slaughtered were those whom Perugia thought could bring a decent ransom, such as the son of the merchant Peter Bernadone.

The dungeon into which Francis was thrown was lit by only a few torches, which still left it dark and did nothing for the dampness that hung heavy in the air. The place smelled of men's sweat, rotting hay and human waste.

But while most prisoners sat dejected, moaning about their state, Francis went about trying to cheer everyone up. He poked fun of his chains and laughed often. When one noble had become so bitter and unbearable that all the prisoners shunned him, Francis befriended him, and orchestrated reconciliation between him and the other prisoners.

Still, the relentless conditions took their toll and sabotaged even Francis's naturally buoyant spirit, and by the time negotiations for his release were arranged (it took

'He [the young Francis] was naturally courteous in manner and speech and, following his heart's intent, never uttered a rude or offensive word to anyone.'

THE LEGEND OF THE THREE COMPANIONS, 1241–47

Previous pages:
On and off
through the
Middle Ages,
tournaments
were the rage
among Europe's
elite, who were
captivated by the
cult of chivalry.
French manuscript
illumination
(c. 1470).

a year, with his father paying a hefty ransom), Francis had become desperately ill. He spent many weeks in bed. When he finally could stand on his own, he was forced to use a cane for weeks.

Knightly ambitions

Francis's illness threw him into an uncharacteristic depression. But soon enough, military ambitions again clouded his mind, and he began planning another expedition. He had heard that an Assisi count named Gentile was preparing to leave for Apulia to engage in another battle between church and empire. Francis convinced the count to let him join him.

Becoming a knight

Before a man could enter knighthood, he had to prove himself worthy in battle and outfit himself in knight's armour. It was the latter requirement that limited knighthood to the nobility and wealthy.

A knight's outfit was enormously expensive. There was the hauberk (a long tunic made of chain mail), the cuisse (plate armour that covered the thighs), the *jambeaux* (armour for below the knees), the *sollerets* (steel shoes) and the helmet. Of course, the potential knight needed a sword, a hilt, a lance (with his pennant on top) and a shield with his coat of arms. On top of all this went the surcoat, a robe which covered the entire man. In addition, the candidate had to own a horse – no small expense – and outfit it with armour, which amounted to chain mail to protect the flanks, and the *chamfron*, armour which covered the front of the head.

To assist him, the knight also had to have a squire, who had to be similarly outfitted.

Once accepted by a sponsor, the candidate for knighthood passed the night in prayer before an altar on which his armour lay. In the morning, he participated in the Mass. On his knees, he took an oath to use his sword to serve God and the oppressed.

After this, his sponsor gave him the accolade, a symbolic blow with the fist on the back of the neck. Finally, the sponsor embraced him, saying, 'In the name of God, of St Michael and of St George, I dub you knight. Be brave, courageous, and loyal.'

He feverishly began making preparations. Though not yet a knight, Francis insisted on looking like one – which cost his father a small fortune – sporting a coat of mail, a helmet, a sword, a lance with its pennant and a flowing robe.

(His father, it turned out, ended up paying for more than his son's outfit. As Francis was making ready for the expedition, he ran across a bedraggled knight with a threadbare outfit. Francis, in a characteristic gesture of generosity, invited the man to dinner and, before the evening was out, had given him a whole new knightly outfit.)

In the midst of his preparations, Francis had a dream. He found himself in his father's house, which had been transformed into a palace filled with arms. Instead of bales of cloths, he saw saddles, shields and lances. In one room, a beautiful bride waited for her bridegroom. Francis heard a voice saying that all this was for Francis and his knights.

When Francis awoke, he was ecstatic. He saw the dream as a portent of the expedition's success and the glory that was eventually to be his. As he bounced around his father's shop the next day, a customer asked him what he was so happy about. 'I know that I will become a great prince!' he replied.

The day to depart arrived, and the 25-year-old Francis, joined by a companion and squire, set off to join Count Gentile. The threesome got as far as Spoleto on the first day.

It turned out to be the last day of their adventure. That night, Francis had another dream, this one deeply troubling. In it, an unknown voice asked him where he wanted to go. When Francis explained his plans, the voice asked, 'Who can do more good for you? The lord or the servant?'

'The lord,' Francis replied.

'Then why', said the voice, 'are you abandoning the lord for the servant, the patron for the client?'

A puzzled Francis asked, 'Lord, what do you want me to do?'

*St Francis Giving
Away His Clothes
and St Francis
Dreaming*
(1437–44) by
Sassetta.

'Go back to your land, and what you are to do will be told to you.'

The next morning, Francis told his companions that he was abandoning the expedition. The dazed trio returned to Assisi immediately.

This mysterious dream, coming on the heels of a humiliating defeat and a year's imprisonment, got Francis's attention. To be sure, the youthful passions were almost impossible to shake off and, for the rest of his life, Francis would be haunted by knightly ambitions. But never again would he don military dress or take up the sword.

C H A P T E R   2

The Hedonist

rancis's re-evaluation of his life had begun in fits and starts, and earlier than his aborted mission to Apulia. As a young man, Francis had been enchanted by the Assisi countryside. His father owned a considerable amount of land outside of town, and Francis would often visit these properties to allow the fields and woods to invigorate him. As his illness from the Perugia imprisonment had abated, he was anxious to take a stroll in the fields below the town. But, to his surprise, the outing proved disappointing. As Thomas of Celano put it, 'But this time, neither the beauty of the fields and the smiling vineyards, nor anything pleasant to the sight was able to charm him.'

Francis was astonished. He began to wonder why he had become so attached to things of this world and,

Risky business

Medieval merchants traded a variety of goods all over Europe and the Middle East. But the most financially rewarding product was cloth. Northern Italian towns produced silk, velvet and brocade and, sometimes woven into the fabric, threads of gold and silver.

Most international trade occurred at large markets, or fairs, held in large towns. The fairs held in Champagne, in eastern France, were the most well known. They were so important to the local economy that the king of France promised safety to merchants who had to cross France to get there. Highway robbery, though, remained a threat.

Because of this, few merchants carried large sums of money, but instead used bills of exchange – a kind of cheque which was recognized in all countries. The first banks arose to help to make such transactions possible.

Despite these precautions, such business still entailed risks. To share the risks, many merchants formed partnerships; one man would put up the money, the other would undertake the dangerous journey to the fair.

'profoundly disillusioned,' says Thomas, 'he sadly returned home'.

But he was still very much taken with things of the world. It would take more than a momentary depression or even one startling dream to completely wake him from his material stupor.

Wealth and business

Francis' father was not as greedy as some early biographers of Francis make him out to be. Still, Peter Bernadone was fond of money, sought public admiration and, like many merchants of Assisi, longed to rise in the social order. He wished nothing less for his son and, for a long time, the wish was coming true.

Peter's business was cloth and, in central Italy, the cloth trade flourished – thanks to peace brought about by

People dying cloth, the commodity from which Francis's father earned his wealth. Fifteenth-century manuscript illumination.

Emperor Frederick Barbarossa, which helped this and other industries to grow. But, wanting to deal in more than coarse Italian wools, Peter often travelled to Provence and Champagne, to fairs where merchants from Europe, Asia and Africa exchanged the finest material then known. Peter did well for himself and his family; he was able to acquire extensive holdings around Assisi, and was a major benefactor to the commune of Assisi.

Naturally, Peter Bernadone's sons, Francis and Angelo, were taught the family business. Growing up, Francis waited on customers, and went on horseback to conduct business in Spoleto and Foligno. He travelled with his father to the fairs in France (which is where he also picked up French). In short, according to biographer Thomas of Celano, Francis too became 'most prudent in business'.

At the same time, he became most profligate in spending. 'He spent so much money on himself and others', says *The Legend of the Three Companions*, 'that he seemed to be the son of some great prince.'

His fondness for parties has already been mentioned, but clothes were another weakness. *The Legend of the Three Companions* notes, 'He was most lavish in spending, so much so that all he could possess and earn was squandered on feasting and other pursuits... spending more money on expensive clothes than his social position warranted.' Sometimes, just to show how much he could afford to squander his resources, he would combine the cheapest cloth with the most expensive materials in the same piece of clothing.

A change of heart

If Francis spent lavishly on himself, he was not hesitant to share his wealth – or, at least, his father's wealth. His outfitting of the bedraggled knight is one example. Another came earlier. Francis was minding his father's shop when a beggar came in and asked for alms, 'for the love of God'. Francis was preoccupied with his work and ignored the man. When the man would not go away,

Francis became impatient and brusquely told him to leave.

As soon as the beggar stepped into the street, Francis regretted his rudeness. 'If that poor man had asked something from you for a great count or baron, you would certainly have granted him his request,' he scolded himself. 'How much more should you have done this for the King of Kings and Lord of Lords.' He rushed out of his shop and gave the man some money. He resolved never again to refuse anyone who begged in the name of God.

This sympathy for the poor may have been learned from his mother, Pica. Legend has it that she came from a distinguished family in France, and most early biographies paint her, in contrast to her husband, as a devout Catholic and 'a friend of all complete integrity'. She is said to have instilled into Francis as many Christian virtues as the young, wild man could absorb. It was not until after his aborted knightly errand to Apulia that some of those virtues began to blossom in Francis, albeit ever so slowly. Still, a change was evident to his friends.

One evening, they arrived at his house, handed him a

'Kids today!'

The sorry state of children and youth was a constant refrain among many medieval writers. For example, Francis's biographer, Thomas of Celano, in *The Life of St Francis*, complained, 'A most wicked custom has been so thoroughly ingrained among those regarded as Christians… as a result, they are eager to bring up their children from the very cradle too indulgently and carelessly… Compelled by the anxiety of youth, they are not bold enough to conduct themselves honourably, since in doing so they would be subject to harsh discipline… But when they begin to enter the gates of adolescence, what sort of individuals do your imagine they become?… Since they are permitted to fulfil every desire, they surrender themselves with all their energy to the service of outrageous conduct.'

Such wholesale condemnations were usually written by men who had voluntarily submitted to the disciplines of the monastic life. In spite of their bias and hyperbole, however, many 13th-century people would have agreed with this description – as would have Francis looking back on his wild youth.

mock sceptre, and announced that they had made him 'king of youth'. What they really wanted was for him to foot the bill for another wild night on the town. Francis obliged, as usual. After a gluttonous banquet, the group spilled out into the Assisi streets, singing drunken refrains late into the night. Francis, sceptre in hand, dragged behind the rest, preoccupied. He found himself strangely bored with the very activity that had formerly given him such pleasure.

Suddenly, while considering the vanity of his life, Francis was filled with an inexplicable sensation. 'He was unable to speak or move,' says *The Legend of the Three Companions*. 'He could only feel and hear this marvellous tenderness', which he attributed to God.

His friends had blithely gone on ahead. When they noticed his absence, they turned around to find him. They found him transfixed, and they began teasing him, asking if he was daydreaming about a woman he might marry. Francis came back in kind: 'You are right! I was thinking about

The medieval town street

The streets of a medieval town were not charming, as we might imagine today. In the daytime, towns were noisy and crowded places. Town criers shouted news of fairs, marriages and opportunities to buy property. Beggars pleaded for handouts. Merchants hawked their wares. Church bells rang throughout the day, announcing services, council meetings, and the start and end of the working day.

Day and night, the streets were a mess. People sometimes threw rubbish and excrement into the street. Few towns could keep up with cleaning the streets. Lincoln, in northern England, smelled so bad that foreign merchants once boycotted the town.

At night, thieves often plied their trade in unlit streets. Some towns hired locals to police the streets, and most towns closed the city gates at night to keep out strangers. Most law-abiding citizens shut their windows and stayed inside for the night.

All of this suggests that Francis and his companions, in going about town at all hours, were not just young men out looking for a good time. They were pushing the edge of what was considered respectable and, perhaps, legal.

taking a wife more noble, wealthier, and more beautiful than you have ever seen.'

Everyone laughed at Francis's characteristic bravado. But a few thought they had detected a change in him. What they did not understand, and what Francis himself still did not fully grasp for years, was that he was speaking of his future marriage to 'Lady Poverty'. Though he still had no idea what all this meant, this much was clear: 'He began to consider himself of little value,' says *The Legend of the Three Companions*, 'and to despise those things which he had previously held in love.'

To work out what was going on inside him, Francis began spending more time with one friend, whom the biographers never name. Together, they would walk outside the city to a certain cave (probably on one of Peter Bernadone's properties), into which Francis would enter to pray, sometimes for hours at a time. He implored God to show him God's will. He trembled as he recalled his sins, and repeatedly repented of them. He worried that he would be unable to resist future temptations.

He suffered such torment inside the cave that, as Thomas of Celano puts it, 'When he came back out, he was so exhausted from his struggle that one person seemed to have entered, and another to have come out.' Francis endured these agonies of conscience for weeks.

And then one day they ended. After he pleaded once more with God, says Thomas, 'The Lord showed him what he must do.' But he still hesitated to speak plainly about what exactly that was. Perhaps he still did not fully know. With friends, he spoke of his 'hidden treasure'. He said that, although he refused to go to Apulia on a knight's errand, he would do great deeds at home. And when people wondered when he was going to take a bride, he spoke again of a mysterious lady who had captured his heart.

A change in behaviour

Slowly, Francis's actions began to make sense of his words. He gave more and more alms to the poor. If he had no

'Many times... having sat down at table, he had barely begun to eat when he would stop eating and drinking, absorbed in meditation on heavenly things.'

DESCRIPTION OF FRANCIS'S SPIRITUAL STATE AFTER THE VISION AT SAN DAMIANO, IN *THE LEGEND OF THE THREE COMPANIONS*, 1241–47

money, he offered them his hat, belt or sometimes the shirt off his back. He purchased communion chalices for local priests. He saved leftovers from dinner for beggars. He also went on a pilgrimage.

It may have been at the suggestion of his friend or a

priestly confessor (perhaps the local bishop). Perhaps it was a spontaneous idea. In any event, Francis walked to Rome with some companions (who, again, remain unnamed) to pray at the plethora of sacred sites there. The experience both scandalized him and changed him even more.

When he visited St Peter's Tomb, he was shocked at the stinginess of pilgrims, most of whom gave but paltry offerings. After watching this for a while, a disgusted Francis pulled a handful of coins from his pocket and threw them at the offering box, hoping that the clanging coins bouncing on the stone floor would shock people into giving more.

At another point, he was so intrigued by the hundreds of beggars who milled about pilgrimage sites that he decided to see what it would feel like to be one of them. He stripped himself of his middle-class attire and donned the rags of a beggar, shared in their meagre meals and walked about with them, begging for alms. His travelling companions soon put a stop to this. But the experience of begging so moved Francis that he began to ponder ever more deeply what was required of him, and what it meant to live a life of poverty.

When he returned to Assisi, he now spent even more time alone. When he did come out in public, he performed even more acts of charity for the poor and with lepers, in what the townspeople increasingly saw as Francis's strange obsession.

The Assisi countryside, like much of Europe, was dotted with chapels, churches and abbeys, each dedicated to one saint or another. Some were well endowed, others neglected, and most had a priest who depended on the generosity of locals to sustain him and the church.

San Damiano, just over a kilometre below Assisi, was such a church. It was guarded by olive trees and had a sweeping view of the wheat fields on the plain below. The church itself was in general disrepair; the walls crumbled all about it, and the priest only eked out an existence. He

Opposite page: The divorce of piety and mercy, which disgusted Francis, is eloquently portrayed in this altarpiece by Sebastiano di Cola.

Francis praying in
the San Damiano
chapel, where he
heard the
decisive words,
'Francis, go and
repair my house,
which you can
see is all being
destroyed.'
Fresco by Giotto
di Bondone.

did not even have enough money to buy oil, let alone a lamp, to burn continually on the altar.

On one of his country walks, Francis decided to step into the chapel. In scattered light, he made his way to the altar, knelt before a painted Byzantine crucifix and began to pray.

How long he prayed and what exactly he said is unclear. But sometime in the middle of his prayer, as Francis gazed at the crucifix, he heard Christ speak from it: 'Francis, go and repair my house, which you can see is all being destroyed.'

Up to this point in his life, Francis had had dreams in which he believed God had spoken to him. He had also felt a sense of God's leading from time to time. But he had never experienced such a direct spiritual communication. He was 'more than a little stunned', as Thomas of Celano notes in *The Remembrance of the Desire of a Soul*, 'trembling and stuttering like a man out of his senses'. He pulled himself up from prayer and then pulled himself together. He vowed to carry out the command as quickly and as literally as he knew how.

The restoration of San Damiano

If Francis had abandoned his quest for knighthood, he did not abandon all knight-like behaviour. In that day, it was not uncommon for a knight to build or restore a chapel, especially if he was anxious to atone for his sins. In a like spirit, Francis began planning the restoration of San Damiano.

First, he needed money, and he knew exactly where to get some. He hurried to his father's shop, gathered up a variety of cloths, especially scarlet (which would fetch a good price). He mounted the family horse and set off for the market in Foligno, about 16 kilometres south. After he had sold all the cloth, he entertained

offers for the horse, and then sold it as well. He walked back to San Damiano, found the priest, kissed his hands and presented him with the day's receipts.

The priest, aware of Francis's playful reputation, thought it a prank. And even if it was not, he was not about to take so much money from the son of Peter Bernadone, the powerful and ill-tempered city father. So the priest declined the offer.

Francis would not be so easily refused, partly because he had decided that he was not going to be weighed down with riches. So he tossed the bag of coins indifferently onto a window sill in the corner of the chapel. If the priest would not accept his money, he asked, would he at least accept the offering of himself? Could he begin living at the chapel and set about repairing it? To this, the priest relented.

A mystified Peter Bernadone, after making inquiries about town, finally worked out what happened to his inventory, his horse and his son. He was furious. He set out for San Damiano immediately to seize Francis and bring him home.

When Francis heard that his father was approaching, he was terrified. He knew that his father would not comprehend his new calling. Francis also knew himself. He knew that he was likely to crumble under his father's wrath and meekly return home. He did not think he could face his father just yet, so he ran. He found refuge in a nearby cave and huddled there for a month, asking God for courage and wisdom.

The crucifix of San Damiano, through which Francis said Christ spoke to him. Romanesque (11th or 12th century).

Facing his father

Francis's cowardice finally abated, and he decided that God had given him no choice but to get back to repairing San Damiano. And that meant first a return to Assisi to beg for more supplies, no matter the consequences, which he knew would be swift and harsh.

His ragged, soiled clothes hung more loosely than ever on his thin frame, and his face was drawn as he made his way through the Assisi streets, boldly asking for alms and supplies. His appearance created quite a stir. Was this not Francis, Peter Bernadone's son? The rascal about town turned thief? His friends were scandalized. Many thought that he had gone mad from starving himself. They mocked him – 'Lunatic!' And when he asked for stones to rebuild the walls of San Damiano, they obliged by throwing them at him, along with handfuls of mud.

Word soon got to Peter Bernadone, who was more horrified than ever. He had spent years building both his business and his reputation; he was finally a respected citizen of the commune. Francis was bringing shame to the Bernadone name, sabotaging all he had worked for these many years. Peter rushed about, desperately searching for his son, and finally found him just as the gossip mill had described him, wretched and a complete embarrassment. In a rage, he grabbed Francis and dragged him home. He beat him, then chained him in the basement. He cursed him, lectured him, and then cursed and lectured him again: Francis was going to stay chained up until he came to his senses, he shouted.

Business commitments soon called Peter away, and it was not long before Francis's mother, more pious than her husband and more sympathetic to Francis's religious awakening, unbound him. Francis headed immediately for San Damiano.

When Peter returned from his business trip and found out what happened, he flew into another rage. Again he stormed off to San Damiano. He bullied and threatened Francis, but this time Francis neither ran nor submitted.

'[Francis's] progression towards a new vocation was slow and halting, subject to certain doubts which persisted throughout his life.'

MICHAEL ROBSON, *ST FRANCIS OF ASSISI: THE LEGEND AND THE LIFE*, 1997

'[Francis] went about by himself collecting stones. He begged all the people he met to give him stones. In fact he became a new sort of beggar, reversing the parable: a beggar who asks not for bread but a stone.'

G.K. CHESTERTON, *ST FRANCIS OF ASSISI*, 1924

Peter rushed back to Assisi and filed a lawsuit against his son, demanding restitution and that his son be banished from the city.

Communal consuls rode down to San Damiano and told Francis he was going to have to appear in court, but again Francis refused. He reminded them that since he was living with a priest at a church, he was under the jurisdiction of the church; secular authorities had no power over him. Not wanting to turn a family matter into a contest of church and state, the consuls told Peter that their hands were tied.

Peter was unrelenting. Surely, he reasoned, the church would not condone thievery, even if done in the name of Christ, and off he went to see the bishop. Bishop Guido was not unsympathetic to Peter. He had earned a reputation as one of the most acquisitive prelates in Italy. He owned even more land in and around Assisi than did Peter. He understood the value of money and the foolishness of squandering resources, no matter what the cause was. So he sent a messenger to San Damiano and told Francis to appear before him.

To this, Francis readily agreed. He knew that, despite the bishop's well-deserved reputation in temporal matters, he was also a man sensitive to things spiritual. Francis had been seeking the bishop's spiritual counsel during the past few months. Francis's reverence for the church, and for its priests and bishops, no doubt deepened through these

Family prisons

Though Peter Bernadone's behaviour is considered abusive today, in medieval Italy, his treatment of his son was legally protected. At the request of just two relatives, any 'dissipater' could be thrown into the commune's prison. If a son, even as an adult, squandered family assets, a father was empowered to have the son imprisoned in the communal jail. Even without proof of charges, communal magistrates had to carry out a father's will in this regard. If a father preferred, he could take care of the matter himself, bind his son in chains and imprison him at home. The records of Assisi suggest that many families had private prisons.

encounters. As Francis put it, he gladly went because the bishop 'is the father and lord of souls'.

The day for the hearing arrived. Both Francis and his father, as well as a handful of spectators, gathered in the piazza of St Mary Major, in front of the bishop's palace. After official preliminaries, Peter rehearsed his complaints: the stolen cloth, selling the family horse and so on.

The matter seemed simple enough to Bishop Guido. 'Your father is infuriated and extremely scandalized,' he said to Francis. 'If you wish to serve God, return the money you have, because God does not want you to spend money unjustly acquired for the work of the church.' He also encouraged him to trust in God: 'He will be your help and will abundantly provide you with whatever is necessary for the work of his church.'

Francis, already showing saintly forbearance, did not even hint at how hypocritical this advice sounded coming from one of Italy's most greedy bishops. He did not chide Guido, nor argue with his father. What he did – and it appears that he had given this next move some forethought – was to use his characteristic flair for the dramatic to make a point which neither his spiritual father nor his natural father would soon forget. 'Lord,' he replied to the bishop, 'I will gladly give back not only the money I acquired from his things.'

He then stepped briefly into the bishop's palace, disrobed and folded his clothes into a neat pile. He stepped back into the piazza, naked. He walked up to his father and presented him with the pile of clothes with a bag of money on top. The shocked observers took in his words: 'Listen to me, all of you, and understand: Until now, I have called Peter Bernadone my father. But, because I have proposed to serve God, I return the money... and all the clothing that is his, wanting to say from now on, "My father who is in heaven," and not "My father, Peter Bernadone."'

While the onlookers watched in stunned silence, Peter fumed. He grabbed the clothes and money, and stormed home. Francis's act of complete devotion could not be read in

Francis's dramatic
rejection of his
father and his
embrace of
poverty are
depicted in
*St Francis
Renounces
His Worldly
Possessions*
by Giotto di
Bondone.

any other way than a deep insult to Peter. If father and son were ever reconciled, the biographers never record it.

The bishop, for his part, was deeply moved by Francis's gesture. Perhaps he understood it as a gentle, but well-deserved rebuke. In any case, he was not put off. Instead, he embraced Francis, took off his velvet mantle and wrapped it around Francis.

Francis, probably both frightened and delighted at the finality of this break, made his way through the streets of Assisi, out of the city gates and down the slope to San Damiano. He had the mantle returned to the bishop and then outfitted himself in the clothes of a hermit – a tunic tied with a leather belt at the waist, sandals and a walking staff. The break with his past was nearly complete.

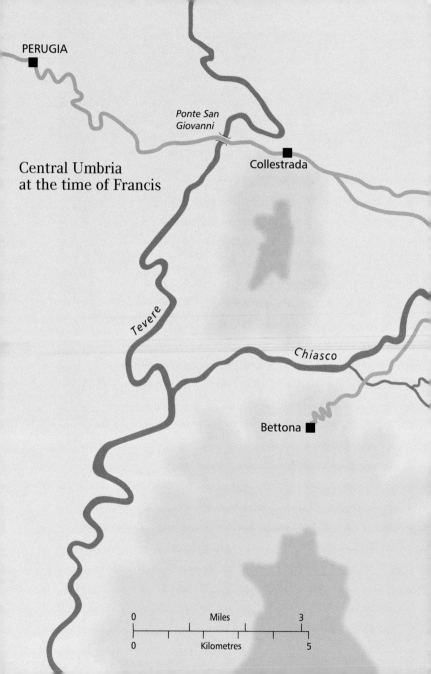

PERUGIA

Ponte San Giovanni

Collestrada

Central Umbria
at the time of Francis

Tevere

Chiasco

Bettona

| 0 | | Miles | | 3 |
| 0 | | Kilometres | | 5 |

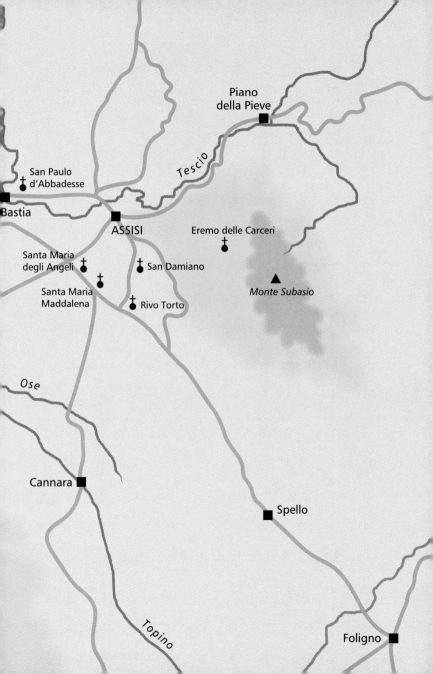

CHAPTER 3

The Reformer

St Rufino (with
the bishop's
mitre) was the
one most
responsible for
converting Assisi
in the third
century, at least
according to the
legends Francis
grew up on.
Fresco from the
school of Giotto
(c. 1320),
Magdalene
Chapel, Basilica
San Francesco,
Assisi.

Church tradition says that Assisi was first evangelized just two decades after Jesus' death and resurrection, by one Crispoldo, said to be a disciple of the apostle Peter. But Assisians usually insist that it was Rufino's heroism two centuries later that converted the town. Francis, like all the children of Assisi, heard gruesome and heroic accounts of saints such as Felicianus, Victorinus and Savinus – third-century Assisi bishops killed for their faith. But no story told was more central to Assisi's identity than that of Rufino.

According to legend, Rufino arrived in Assisi and began preaching the message of Christ. The Roman proconsul Aspasio, hearing that another sovereignty was being proclaimed in his district, ordered the troublemaker to appear before him and told him to cease preaching – or else he would be forced to apply the usual punishments. Rufino, unfazed, replied, 'I fear neither you nor your emperors.'

So the proconsul ordered that a lead-tipped whip be applied to Rufino's back, and when that did not change Rufino's mind, he ordered that Rufino be stoned, and told the assailants to aim for his mouth. Still he refused to abandon his call.

Then the story has it that he was thrown into a flaming furnace as the proconsul taunted, 'Let us see if your god knows how to liberate you from my hands' – at which point an angel appeared and guided Rufino out of the flames. The hardened proconsul would not be defeated, and finally ordered, 'Tie a great rock about his neck and throw him into water so deep that the Christians cannot retrieve him.'

Rufino was drowned in the Chiascio River but, despite the proconsul's wish, Christians recovered his body and buried it, oddly enough, in a nearby temple dedicated to Diana. But Rufino's witness had proven effective, impressing enough people to mean that, slowly, the Christian faith took root in the region. By 412, as the Roman Empire was converting to Christianity, Rufino's memory was so revered that his body was exhumed and carried into the city in solemn assembly.

Such examples of unwavering devotion – courageous faith which resulted in the conversion of entire regions – were rehearsed in story and pageant on saints' days, and gave everyone in town pause for thought. This was especially true of Francis after he began re-evaluating his life. His conversion, he slowly realized, was not just about his own soul's salvation but also about the renewal of the entire church.

Self-examination

For a long time, Francis wrestled with his own soul, keeping the pressure on himself to convert more and more of his life. He soon concluded that it was not just ambition and pleasure that he had to give up. God wanted his very self, given with abandon. Nothing revealed this to him more than his neurotic fears.

He went through a period, for example, when he was obsessed with an old Assisi woman who carried a grotesque hump on her back, whose looks scared everyone. Francis got it into his mind – a suggestion of the devil, he later concluded – that if he did not abandon his spiritual quest, he would end up like this woman. The idea filled him with dread, pestering him throughout the day, forcing him to his knees in prayer. He finally found relief one day when he sensed God telling him, 'If you want to know me, despise yourself. For when the order is reversed,

'Francis had set out to win his spurs but had relinquished his buckler and sword, had come of age but abandoned his birthright, and his "richest and most beautiful bride" had turned out to be Lady Poverty.'

ADRIAN HOUSE,
*FRANCIS OF ASSISI:
A REVOLUTIONARY
LIFE,* 2000

the things I say will taste sweet to you even though they seem the opposite.'

However, a bigger fear still blocked Francis's spiritual progress. As he put it years later in *The Testament*, shortly before his death, as a young man, 'It seemed too bitter for me to see lepers.'

On his frequent trips through the countryside, Francis had had many opportunities to run into lepers, and he did everything in his power to avoid them. 'The sight of lepers was so bitter to him that he refused not only to look at them, but even to approach their dwelling,' says *The Legend of the Three Companions*. If he felt moved to give alms, he would only do so through an intermediary and, even then, 'He always turned away his face and held his nose.'

While praying during the early months of his conversion, he believed that he heard this response: 'Francis, everything you loved carnally and desired to have, you must despise and hate if you wish to know my will. Because once you begin doing this, what before seemed delightful and sweet will be

Leprosy

Leprosy was still a not uncommon disease in medieval Europe, and once a person was afflicted with the disease – characterized by decaying flesh, ulcers and loss of feeling – he or she was socially isolated. Below Assisi, there were at least six lazar houses (so named after the biblical Lazarus, who in Jesus' parable was covered with sores – Luke 16:19–31). At San Lazzaro d'Arce, lepers were formally admitted by a priest. The leper stood in the cemetery while the priest pronounced him dead to the world, adding that this life's sufferings would lead him to the kingdom of heaven.

After sprinkling graveyard dust on the leper's head, the priest reminded him of the rules governing lepers. They could not leave the house unless they wore their distinctive grey cloak and sounded their wooden clapper to warn off other travellers. They were forbidden from attending fairs, markets, mills and farms, and from entering Assisi. They could beg for food only if they wore gloves and used a bowl to receive the offerings. They were forbidden from drinking directly from springs, rivers and wells (they could drink only from their own flasks). If they spoke with healthy individuals, they had to stand downwind from them.

unbearable and bitter, and what before made you shudder will offer you great sweetness and enormous delight.'

A little while later, Francis was riding his horse near Assisi (apparently this took place before the rift with his father) when he saw ahead of him a leper standing in the road. He determined immediately to do something sweeping, something dramatic to change his attitude. He dismounted, walked up to the man and personally handed him a coin. But this still was not enough to a man of Francis's resolve. So he bent over, drew his lips near the man's decaying hand and kissed it. The man replied by giving Francis a kiss of peace; Francis did not recoil. Then Francis remounted his horse and went on his way.

Francis, though, went further still. To continue to purge his revulsion of lepers, he moved in among them for a time, distributing alms and kissing the hand of each until 'what before had been bitter… was turned into sweetness'.

This was how Francis slowly conquered his fears, which he saw stood in the way of complete abandonment to God.

Francis bathes lepers – sufferers forsaken by the rest of his society. Altar panel attributed to Bonaventura Berlinghieri in the Bardi chapel, Santa Croce, Florence.

Such experiences showed him that divine revelations and extraordinary dreams were not enough. Spiritual experiences actually changed Francis little, except to give him a broad sense of direction in which to take his life. It was his stubborn determination – energized by God's grace, he would say – to do God's bidding, no matter the cost, that completed his conversion.

Begging

After Francis heard Christ say to him, 'Francis, go and repair my house, which you can see, is all being destroyed,' Francis began going about Assisi and the vicinity, begging for donations for the repair of San Damiano. 'Whoever gives me a stone will receive a reward from the Lord!' he shouted. 'Whoever gives me three will receive three rewards!'

Francis was completely taken with his new project, as much as he had been when he had partied late into the night with friends. While begging for, or working on, San Damiano, he would sometimes break out in song in praise of God. From the scaffold he had constructed around the church, he would joyously assault passers-by, inviting them to help.

The San Damiano priest – the same one who rejected Francis's first monetary offering – soon warmed up to his crazy benefactor and, as poor as he was, began preparing meals for Francis. But Francis, after accepting the first few offerings graciously, felt uncomfortable. 'This is not the life of someone professing poverty!' he scolded himself. 'Get up, stop being lazy, and beg scraps from door to door.'

So Francis went through town, collecting leftovers into a large bowl. After collecting what amounted to so much garbage, he sat down to eat it, as he had vowed he would. But when he looked at the scraps before him, he immediately became nauseous. He paused, took a deep breath, forced the refuse into his mouth and swallowed hard. He later said that, to his surprise, it tasted better than the fine food he had enjoyed in his home. After that, he never let the priest cook for him again.

'[Medieval] hospitals... cathedrals and monasteries were often the "remorse in stone" by means of which great sinners attempted to atone for their crimes and violence.'

OMER ENGLEBERT,
ST FRANCIS OF ASSISI: A BIOGRAPHY, 1965

Outwardly, Francis appeared to accept the humility that begging demanded. But he admitted later that, during this time, he continued to wrestle with his pride. Once, as he went about begging for oil for the San Damiano chapel lamp, he approached a celebration in progress. He noticed that among the merrymakers were some old friends and, before they saw him, he ducked into an alley and started to slink back to San Damiano. But his pride was soon checked by his stubborn piety. He turned around and boldly stepped into their midst. He not only asked them for oil, but he also told them what he had just done and accused himself of cowardice before them.

Throughout his life, in fact, this ironic and very human pattern continued. Francis would deal a blow to one form of pride – in this case, shame before friends at doing what he felt God had called him to do – but he would feel compelled to point out his flaw publicly, thus drawing attention to his new-found humility! What he never seemed to realize was that this was a new form of pride, perhaps even more spiritually dangerous. Francis was indeed a saint, but a saint with ongoing character flaws.

A larger mission
When he had completed the repairs at San Damiano, Francis started work upon another local dilapidated chapel, St Peter's, and then another still, St Mary of the Angels (Santa Maria degli Angeli). It was only slowly, as he worked on these churches and as disciples started to attach themselves to him, that he began to realize his larger mission.

That the medieval church was in need of repair went without saying, though many, including the pope, were not reluctant to say it. At the Fourth Lateran Council, Pope Innocent III noted and condemned a variety of abuses prevalent throughout Europe:

Many priests have lived luxuriously. They have passed the time in drunken revels, neglecting religious rites. When they have been at Mass, they have chatted about commercial affairs.

*They have left churches and tabernacles in an indecent state,
sold posts and sacraments, promoted ignorant and unworthy
people to the clerical state, thought they had others better
suited for it. Many bishops have appropriated the income of a
parish for themselves, leaving the parish indigent. They have
gone to the enormous abuse of forcing parishioners to make
special payments so as to have still more income. They have
extorted money from the faithful on every pretext. They have
made a scandalous commerce of relics. They have allowed the
illegitimate children of a canon to succeed the father in the
benefice.*

*'Woe to all
nations for the
world has
become
darkness! The
Lord's vineyard
has perished;
the Head of the
Church is sick,
and his
members are
dead. Do you
sleep, shepherds
of the flock?'*

ELIZABETH OF
SCHÖNAU (1126–64),
LIBER VIARUM DEI

Assisi knew of such abuses first-hand, especially in the
administration of its highest ranking cleric, Bishop Guido.
The region under his jurisdiction was characterized by
litigation and libel, pronouncements and sentences, as
he sought land, goods and services 'for the diocese'. In
1216, he quarrelled long and viciously with the Benedictine
monks of Monte Subiaso, claiming jurisdiction over some
of their churches. In another dispute, Guido went down
to the piazza and came to blows with an antagonist. On
several occasions, the pope had to step in and reprimand
Guido for his greed.

Consequently, not even Guido's closest colleagues,
the prior and canons of the cathedral, trusted him, let
alone respected him. One part of the compromise reached
after a dispute between Guido and his canons hints at
how fractured the relationship had become: 'The prior and
canons shall promise the bishop obedience and shall observe
the reverence due him.' It goes on to mention that they had
been quarrelling over the power of appointments, the right
to certain offerings and so on. There is no indication that
this compromise permanently healed the rift.

Corruption infected all levels of the church's life.
Priors and canons regularly went to court to argue about
fields and olive groves. Small monasteries rebelled against
the rule of larger monasteries, sometimes each hiring
mercenaries to insist, militarily, on their own way. In short,

the litany of priestly abuses outlined by Innocent III could all be found in Assisi.

Though the abuses were transparent, the solution was not. Innocent III thought it 'would take fire and sword to cure it'. A number of ideas had been and were being tried by sundry prophets and reformers.

Reforming groups

In general, medieval reformers fell into one heresy or another, but one who seemed to start out solidly orthodox was Peter Valdes (1140–1218), who founded the 'Poor Men of Lyons'. Valdes (sometimes written as Waldo) was a wealthy merchant who sold his possessions and lived in voluntary poverty, preaching the gospel. His Bible-based preaching soon won him adherents, who together vowed to live in poverty, penance and perfect equality.

Peter Valdes, a proto-Protestant reformer of the Middle Ages.

The church viewed all this with only mild suspicion until the group began lashing out at the failings of the clergy. The Archbishop of Lyon then excommunicated them. The group appealed to Pope Alexander III (who reigned in 1159–81) to hear their case. In the end, he praised their poverty and authorized them to preach morals to the people – only if the local bishop permitted, and only if they did not try to interpret scripture or teach theology.

Alexander's admonishes fell on deaf ears. The group went out and, acting according to conscience, did as they had always done. Finally, Pope Lucius III (who reigned in 1181–85) condemned them in 1184, when Francis was one year old. One thing led to another, and the greater part of the Waldensians (as they came to be called) began placing the authority of the Bible above the church, and rejected purgatory, indulgences and the veneration of saints. But a minority submitted to the pope, taking on the name 'Poor Catholics' (one historian called them 'pre-Franciscans'). They stopped disparaging priests, lived in poverty, tried to convert heretics, kept two Lents a year, and prayed the 'Our Father' and 'Hail Mary' seven times a day.

The *Humiliati* was another reform-minded group of the era. They, too, were looked upon with suspicion by church authorities, but Pope Innocent III approved them in 1201. They took their name from the ash-grey habit they wore. They were composed of three orders: one of brothers, one of sisters and one of 'seculars'. The latter order comprised people who lived in the world with their families, while dressing modestly, serving the poor, fasting twice a week and saying seven 'Our Fathers' a day. Those in the other two orders ('the religious') lived in convents, performed manual labour, chanted the divine office and, if needed, went out begging to supply their needs. They arose in Lombardy, and within 15 years of their papal approval they already had 150 communities within the Milan diocese alone.

One reform group had the most notorious reputation in Francis's time. They were called the Patarini in Italy, the Albigensians in France and the Bogomiles in Eastern Europe. Mostly they are known as the Cathari.

They believed that two eternal principles competed for pre-eminence. One – God – was the author of all good and of all spiritual souls. The other – Satan or Jehovah – was the author of evil, suffering and all material things, including the human body. Human beings, composed of both soul and flesh, were the product of both principles. Christ came to liberate the spirit from the flesh. He took on human form merely to convince enslaved human beings to rebel against Satan and his church – the Church of Rome – and to bring people to the true church, the church of the Cathari – 'the pure' (from the Greek *katharos*).

This church developed rival priests (or the 'perfect'), a liturgy, parishes, schools and even a few convents. The Cathari had an evangelistic fervour: some became merchants so that they could preach at fairs; others became teachers to influence youth; and others still became doctors to minister

End-times prophet

The most widely influential prophet/reformer of the Middle Ages was a Cistercian monk called Joachim of Fiore (1145–1202). His mathematical analysis of the Bible led him to conclude that history was divided into three periods, represented by the Father, Son and Holy Spirit. The first was an era of law (obedience and fear) and the second was an era of grace (obedience in faith). The third would inaugurate an era of liberty and love.

This cosmology would have been dismissed as the ravings of a religious lunatic if Joachim did not live such an exemplary life. He was gentle and morally pure, and he exhibited a fiery passion for Christ. He basked in the wonders of the created order. He ministered to the dying by letting them spend their last moments lying against his breast. He lived in complete poverty – a marked departure from so many clerics and monks of the day. His teachings inspired thousands, not only to anticipate the millennium but also to shape their lives after his radical example.

The Annunciation to St Joachim, a Hungarian painting from c. 1450.

to the sick and dying. Their preachers lashed out at the immorality of Catholic clergy, denied the efficacy of the sacraments and taught that the laying on of hands was enough to save a soul – assuming that one remained pure afterwards (which is why most Cathari delayed the ceremony until on their death beds). They denounced marriage and seemed indifferent about sexual morals (for the flesh meant nothing if the spirit was holy).

They could be found in many Italian cities, including Rome, and even dominated some towns. They were finally subdued only when church and state joined hands in a crusade against them. After the bloody Albigensian War of 1209, in which thousands of Cathari were ruthlessly slaughtered in southern France, it was just too risky to become a Cathar, and the sect slowly died out. But the lessons for the reform-minded such as Francis were obvious: if you wished to make a difference, you must stay within the bounds of church teaching and clerical authority.

An epiphany

Larger church reform, then, was in the air that Francis breathed, but such a large scheme did not inspire him until he experienced what he believed was another divine revelation.

It happened at the third church which Francis restored. It was legally owned by the Benedictine Abbey of Monte Subiaso, but except for the occasional Mass said there by a visiting priest, the chapel was neglected and in serious disrepair. Francis fell in love with the chapel almost

Francis's treasured chapel, the Portiuncula, now swallowed up inside the Basilica of St Mary of the Angels, built in 1569.

immediately. It was secluded, located in the midst of a quiet forest. The chapel, though nicknamed the Portiuncula (the 'Little Portion') was officially dedicated to St Mary of the Angels, and thus, because of Francis's devotion to Mary, became a much-favoured place.

During a Mass held in honour of St Matthias at the end of February 1208, something extraordinary happened. As the priest read from chapter 10 of the Gospel of Matthew, in which Jesus instructs his disciples to go out and preach, the verses seemed to leap out at Francis: 'You received without payment: give without payment. Take no gold, or silver or copper in your belts, no bag for your journey, or two tunics, or sandals or a staff.'

Francis was mesmerized. After Mass, he rushed up to the priest and begged him to explain. The priest went over the passage line by line, adding parallel readings from the Gospels of Mark and Luke. He explained that Christ's disciples were not to possess gold or silver, nor any money at all for that matter, nor carry a wallet or a sack, nor bread, nor a staff, nor to have shoes and no more than one tunic, so that they could preach the kingdom of God and penance.

An overwhelmed Francis blurted out, 'This is what I want! This is what I seek, this is what I desire with all my heart!' Francis was flooded with joy. He immediately went about changing his ways even more. He exchanged his traditional hermit's garb for something even simpler. He took off his sandals, cast aside his staff and replaced his tunic with something much coarser ('so that in it he might crucify the flesh, with its vices and sins', notes Thomas of Celano in *The Life of St Francis*). Then he put on it the sign of cross ('so that in it, he would drive off every fantasy of the demons', records Thomas) and, instead of a leather belt, he girded himself with a simple rope.

He committed these passages of scripture to memory and, as Thomas notes, 'was careful to carry it out to the letter'. Francis had discovered not only what he was to do with his personal life, but he now also had a concrete method for rebuilding the church.

CHAPTER 4

Little Brothers

U p to this point, Francis's conversion had been mostly a private affair, watched with dismay or amusement by those who knew him. So far, nothing that Francis had done or said inspired anyone but himself. As he became increasingly captivated by the idea of rebuilding the medieval church, that would soon change.

He began by preaching, first in the Church of San

The cathedral of San Rufino, in Assisi, where Francis often preached.

Giorgio, in which he had gone to school as a child, and later in the cathedral of San Rufino. He usually preached on Sundays, spending Saturday evenings devoted to prayer and meditation, reflecting on what he would say to the people the next day.

Francis also travelled the area with his message, sometimes preaching in up to five villages a day. He often preached outdoors, since many priests refused him permission to preach in their churches. In the countryside, Francis often spoke from a bale of straw or from a granary doorway. In the towns, he climbed on a box or up steps in front of a public building. He preached to serfs and their families as well as to the landholders, to merchants, women, clerks and priests – to any who gathered to hear him.

He began each sermon with a salutation, 'May the Lord give you peace.' In an era when war was chivalrous and blood vendettas common, when legal mutilations and

Medieval meeting-houses

Like the New England meeting-houses of the 17th century, the medieval church was more than a place where believers gathered for worship. It also served as community centre. In medieval society, no line separated religious and public life. Before the altar, communal assemblies gathered, heated public debates raged and important ceremonies were performed. Troops came together and prayed here before and after battle. Here, officials conducted legal transactions – deeds and contracts were signed, and the sentences of judges and consuls were announced. In short, it was the ideal place for an aspiring reformer to begin preaching his message.

murder were a part of everyday life, this greeting would have startled listeners.

They were also startled that he was preaching in Italian. Most famous preachers, such as Bernard of Clairvaux, had preached in Latin to win the respect of the educated elite. When preachers did use the local language, they often obscured their message with theological abstractions. Francis co-opted the techniques of the troubadours, making full use of poetic language and images that would drive a message home. When he described the nativity, listeners felt as if Mary was giving birth before their eyes. In rehearsing the crucifixion, the crowd, as well as Francis himself, would shed tears.

From his mouth flowed both kindness and severity. One moment, he was friendly and cheerful; he would sometimes prance about as if he were playing a fiddle on a stick, or break out in song in praise to God and his creation. In another moment, he would turn fiery: 'He denounced evil whenever he found it,' wrote one early biographer, 'and made no effort to palliate it; from him a life of sin met with outspoken rebuke, not support. He spoke with equal candour to great and small.'

All in all, listeners felt as if something radically anew was afoot – the beginning of a religious awakening. Though

'His words were neither hollow nor ridiculous, but filled with the power of the Holy Spirit, penetrating the marrow of the heart, so that listeners were turned to great amazement.'

THE LEGEND OF THE THREE COMPANIONS, 1241–47

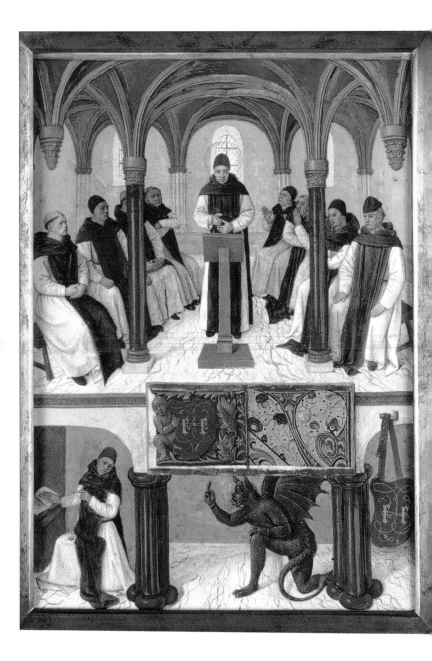

all of society believed in God, when Francis spoke, it was as if God was real for the first time. As a result, 'Some men began to be moved to do penance by his example,' says *The Legend of the Three Companions*, 'and leaving all things, they joined him in life and habit.'

The first followers

Francis's first disciple was a man who followed only for a time before he returned to his previous life. The second follower, and the first to stay the course, was Bernard of Assisi. A rich and powerful lord, Bernard was so taken with Francis's words and conduct that he wondered if he should abandon his well-heeled life. He invited Francis to spend the night in his home to discuss the matter. They prayed together and talked long into the night.

At one point, Bernard asked, 'If, for many years, someone holds on to the possessions, many or few, he has acquired from his lord, and no longer wishes to keep them, what is the better thing for him to do?'

Francis said that he must give them all back to the lord from whom he received them.

Bernard replied, 'Then, brother, I want to give away all my worldly goods for the love of my Lord who gave them to me, as it seems best to you.'

'We will go to the church early in the morning,' Francis said, 'and through the book of the Gospels, we will learn how the Lord instructed his disciples.'

In the morning, they found another man, Peter Cantanii, who had also shown interest in Francis's way of life. Together, they went to the Church of San Nicolò next to the piazza. They immediately found the missal to look up the passage about renunciation. Francis, with dramatic flare, decided to drive home his vision to his potential disciples. He paused for prayer before he opened the book, and then, seemingly at random, his eyes fell on a saying of Jesus: 'If you wish to be perfect, go, sell everything you possess and give to the poor, and you will have treasure in heaven.'

Francis then opened to another passage, and then

Opposite page: Francis, who preached in the vernacular, had a greater following than even the famous St Bernard of Clairvaux, one of the most eloquent of medieval preachers, shown here preaching and resisting temptation. Manuscript illumination (c. 1415/20) by Jean Fouquet.

Downward mobility

The exaltation of poverty was not a new idea by the time of Francis. It began with Jesus, whom Francis liked to quote on the matter: 'None of you can become my disciple if you do not give up all your possessions' (Luke 14:33). Acquiring and caring for material possessions (which Jesus called 'mammon') distracts one from complete devotion to God. Hence Jesus' famous saying, 'You cannot serve God and mammon.'

This emphasis on poverty was muted, however, until the third and fourth centuries, when thousands of hermits, such as Antony of Egypt, sold their possessions and lived on bare essentials in order to give themselves fully to God. The monastic movements inspired by these early hermits – those of Basil in the East and Benedict in the West, among others – included poverty as one of their principal vows.

The fascination with poverty ebbed and flowed, but in the 11th and 12th centuries, a new wave of reformers began to yearn for the 'perfect life' of 'evangelical poverty'. They meant the life of poverty as practised by Christ and the early apostles.

This was partly a reaction to growing materialism. Towns flourished; a new class of merchants (such as Francis's father) were growing wealthy, and the gap between the wealthy and the poor was widening. Reforming monks and itinerant preachers spoke against greed and exploitation, especially against the rising practice of lending money out at interest – the sin of usury. Evangelical poverty was an act of penitence for such sins, as well as an attempt to imitate the life of Christ.

another. Each time a saying of Jesus came immediately into focus. One began, 'Take nothing for your journey...' and another, 'If any want to become my followers, let them deny themselves...'

Francis was already familiar with such passages and had been seeking to carry them out, literally. The triple gesture, which early biographers credited to miracle, seems instead to be Francis's dramatic way of impressing these two men with a theme that had captivated him. Francis concluded, 'Brothers, this is our life and rule, and that of all who will want to join our company. Go, therefore, and fulfil what you have heard.'

Both Bernard and Peter were smitten. Francis's vision seemed to strike at the heart of so much that was wrong with the church and the world. They each sold their possessions, gave the money to the poor and began living with Francis at the Portiuncula.

A hippocentaur speaks to St Antony of the Desert (c. 251–356), the first Christian monk and an inspiration for later ascetics like Francis. French manuscript illumination (c. 1412).

North and
central Italy
at the time
of Francis

Verona Padua Venice

Parma

LOMBARDY

Bologna

Ravenna

ROMANIA

Rimini

San Marino

Monte La Verna San Leo

Pisa

Arno Florence

Poggibonsi

Arezzo

Siena Cortona

Lake Trasimeno

Perugia

Assisi

Ancona

PENTAPOLIS

MARCHES
OF
ANCONA

Gubbio

Ascoli

Foligno

Spoleto

TUSCANY

DUCHY OF SPOLETO

Orvieto

Lake Bolsena

Terni

Narni

Rieti

KINGDOM
OF
SICILY

Tiber (Tevere)

Viterbo

PAPAL STATES

Rome

Cassin

One day, while Bernard distributed the proceeds of the sale of some of his goods, a priest named Sylvester approached Francis. Francis had purchased stones from Sylvester, on credit, to repair San Damiano.

'You did not completely pay me for the stones which you bought from me!' Sylvester complained.

Francis immediately reached into Bernard's pocket and drew out a fistful of coins and handed them to Sylvester. 'Do you now have full payment, Lord Priest?'

An overjoyed Sylvester replied, 'I have it completely, brother,' and hurried home.

But, over the next few days, Sylvester found that he could not live with himself. 'Am I not a miserable man?' he said to himself. 'Old as I am, don't I still covet and desire things of this world? And this young man despises and scorns them all for the love of God!'

He would continue to wrestle with himself like this for months before finally joining Francis.

Meanwhile, Francis, Bernard and Peter set up quarters in the dilapidated St Mary of the Angels, three kilometres below Assisi. This was where Francis had been mesmerized by the Gospel reading about poverty. The Benedictines who owned the grounds were happy to have guests to take care of the place. So the three built a little hut – a primitive affair of branches, sticks, reeds and clay – to live in while they worked on the chapel. A week later, a young farmer named Giles joined this new community. By late April in 1208, four small seeds of new life for the church had been sown.

Spreading out

Sometime during the next few weeks, Francis divided the group into two. He sent Bernard and Peter in one direction, while he and Giles set off for the Marches of Acona. Francis's ambition to do something glorious with his life was still very much part of him, but he was channelling that ambition to more noble ends. He told Giles, 'Our religion [meaning their way of life] will be like a fisherman who casts his nets into the water catching a great number of fish, and, leaving the

'Throughout his life from now on Francis emanated an almost radioactive energy which seemed to derive from his sense of continuous proximity to God.'

ADRIAN HOUSE,
FRANCIS OF ASSISI: A REVOLUTIONARY LIFE, 2000

small ones in the water, he puts the large ones into his basket.'

As they walked, Francis played the joyful troubadour of the Lord. He went about singing, as *The Legend of the Three Companions* records, 'with a loud and clear voice, in French, the praises of the Lord, blessing and glorifying the goodness of the most high'.

He encouraged listeners to fear and love God, and to do penance for their sins. Some hearers thought of Giles and Francis as fools or drunkards. Others reasoned, 'Either they cling to the Lord for the sake of the highest perfection, or they are demented for sure, because their life seems reckless. They use little food, walk barefoot, and wear wretched clothes.' Young women, startled by the brothers' seeming madness, ran when they saw them coming.

But when all four returned to the Portiuncula, four more men asked to join the band. With that, the people of Assisi become concerned. To have Francis and one or two men live an eccentric life at the edge of town was one thing. To be the centre of a growing movement, one that often came into town begging – well, that was another. They ignored the brothers when they begged for food and building supplies. They mocked them for ridding themselves of their possessions and living off others. Even their families called them senseless and stupid.

Bishop Guido, to whom Francis often went for advice, decided to intervene. His first response was to try to convince Francis to moderate his lifestyle. He should take on a few possessions so that his brothers would not have to beg so much. 'It seems to me that your life is very rough and hard,' the bishop explained, 'especially in not possessing anything in this world.'

'Lord, if we had possessions, we would need arms for our protection,' he replied. 'For disputes and lawsuits usually arise out of them, and, because of this, love of God and neighbour are greatly impeded. Therefore, we do not want to possess anything in this world.'

That Francis actually got away with this is surprising. It is a testimony to his winsomeness. He was making a jab at the bishop's lifestyle, but the bishop did not seem to mind.

Penance and forgiveness

During this period, Francis was stricken with another bout of conscience. He was assaulted by memories of the sins of his youth, his years of vanity and greed. He was filled with guilt and dread for his soul. He kept repeating the phrase, 'Lord, be merciful to me, a sinner.' But darkness and fear continued to engulf him.

One day, as he repeated the prayer, though, an 'indescribable joy and tremendous sweetness began to well up in his heart', writes Thomas of Celano in *The Life of St Francis*. 'He began to lose himself. His feelings were pressed together, and that darkness disappeared.'

Suddenly, a new certainty about the forgiveness of his sins poured into him. He felt himself engulfed in light, and he saw much more clearly the future that lay before him. Thomas writes, 'He now seemed to be changed into another man.'

It was now autumn 1208, just a few months after Bernard and Peter had joined Francis. Francis was now emboldened to send the brothers out two by two to even more distant reaches. He told them to consider their mutual calling: 'To go throughout the world, encouraging everyone, more by deed than by word, to do penance for their sins and to recall the commandments of God.'

Despite the modern temptation to sentimentalize Francis and his mission, he did not send his brothers out, on this occasion or ever, to proclaim a saccharine message about God's love and the wonder of creation. In an early guide written during this period, Francis instructs his brothers to tell their listeners, 'Do penance, performing worthy fruits of penance, because we shall soon die... Blessed are those who die in penance for they shall be in the kingdom of heaven. Woe to those who do not die in penance, for they shall be children of the devil whose works they do and they shall go into everlasting fire.'

Francis warned his brothers about the hostility they were likely to meet, but told them that they were not to be afraid. It would not be long before 'many learned and noble men will come to us, and will be with us preaching to kings and rulers and great crowds'. Many would be converted, he concluded, adding confidently that God would 'multiply and increase his family throughout the entire world'.

He then blessed them and sent them out. He added one other point of instruction. Whenever they happened upon a cross or church, they were to pray, 'We adore you, Christ, and we bless you in all your churches throughout the whole world, because by your holy cross, you have redeemed the world.'

Again, the reception for the brothers was mixed. Their dress and way of life amazed people. They 'seemed almost like wild men', says *The Legend of the Three Companions*. Some received their message, and others mocked them. Others still asked where they came from, and which order they belonged to. They replied that they were penitents from Assisi and that, no, they were not an official order of the church.

At the end of each day, they sought lodging, but few people trusted them into their homes. They were forced to sleep in porticos in churches and homes. Since this mission was conducted in the autumn and winter, this meant some cold, sleepless nights.

One memorable exception was Bernard's and Giles's experience in Florence (on their way to St James of Compostela). At the end of a long day of preaching and begging, they came across a portico that had an oven. They received permission from woman of the house to sleep by the oven. When her husband found these strangers in the portico, he scolded his wife and called the men 'scoundrels and thieves'. Still, she managed to convince him that they could do no harm where they lay.

The next morning, Bernard and Giles went to church,

as was their custom, and the wife secretly followed them. She watched them as they prayed with evident devotion, and then as a man offered, and they refused, alms. 'While it is true that we are poor, poverty is not burdensome for us,' said Bernard. 'For by the grace of God we have willingly made ourselves poor.' Now thoroughly convinced of their sincerity, the women rushed up and invited them to stay in her home – again to the dismay of her husband.

Still, more times than not, people abused them.

Penance

Francis was not alone in highlighting penance. Many reform movements of the era, such as the *Humiliati* of Italy, were known as penitents, as were Francis and his followers.

Francis wanted his followers to practise both the sacrament and virtue of penance. In the sacrament (still practised today in Roman Catholicism), the penitent confessed his sins to a priest, received absolution and performed acts which satisfied the holy demands of the Law. This delivered the sinner from the temporal punishments due to sin (eternal punishments being remitted at absolution).

The virtue of penance was a heartfelt sorrow for sin, even the hating of one's sin, a necessary condition for the expiation of sin. But, in either case, it entailed concrete acts: prayers, fasting and sometimes self-flagellation. But it also meant such things as giving alms to the poor and reconciling oneself with one's enemies.

As the Middle Ages progressed, the practice of penance slipped into an exacting and oppressive legalism. But early on, most people thought of it as liberating. Theologically, every medieval Christian knew the utter holiness of God and the utter depravity of humankind. Human sin could hardly be atoned for by mere contrition and acts of satisfaction. The offence to God's perfection was too great. Yet God's mercy made forgiveness possible again. Because of Christ's sacrificial death on the cross, God commissioned the church to forgive sins through the sacrament of penance.

At times, Francis seemed caught between the two. Sometimes he saw penance as liberating; at other times, he seemed to use it as a legalist stick to keep his friars in order. It was a tension that neither he nor the Middle Ages ever resolved.

Sometimes, angry crowds would strip the tunics off their backs. Since they had vowed, according to Jesus' command, to give to anyone who asked and to ask for nothing in return, and to go about with only one tunic, they were sometimes left semi-naked in the street. On top of that, and according to another command of Jesus, they prayed for their persecutors.

Slowly, people came to respect their gracious steadfastness in the face of abuse, their refusal to handle money, the patience with which they bore suffering (one story tells of how they left footprints of blood in the snow as they journeyed barefoot). And people could not get over the joy with which they carried themselves and preached their message. Some actually came up to them and asked forgiveness for mistreating them. Others came up and asked to join them.

When they returned to the Portiuncula in early 1209, another four joined the band, bringing the total to a biblical 12. They felt that they were the Lord's disciples for a new era. Their enthusiasm for their way of life seemed to know no bounds.

One day as two of them walked along the road, a man began throwing stones at one of them. The other immediately put himself in the path of the stones to spare his brother.

If one happened to utter an annoying word to another, his conscience so troubled him that he could not rest until he admitted the fault. He would lay prostrate on the floor, asking the offended brother to place his foot over his mouth. If they saw a beggar and had nothing to give him, they would often tear off a portion of their own tunics and give them to the man.

They sought complete devotion to God, which meant in their minds a complete break with their families. They even avoided visiting areas where relatives lived, so that they could observe the prophetic psalm, 'I have become a stranger to my kindred, an alien to my mother's children' (Psalm 69:8).

Such acts were not the morbid gestures of the seriously self-righteous. They would never have attracted the numbers they eventually did. All this piety was imbued with a sense of joy at feeling that they had given themselves completely to a gracious and loving Lord.

As *The Legend of the Three Companions* puts it, 'They constantly rejoiced in the Lord, not having within themselves nor among themselves anything that could make them sad. For the more they were separated from the world, the more they were united to God. As they advanced on the way of the cross and the paths of justice, they cleared all hindrances from the narrow path of penance and of the observance of the gospel.'

CHAPTER 5

The Order's Founding

*'Beware of pride
and vainglory.
Let us guard
ourselves from
the wisdom of
this world and
the prudence
of the flesh.'*

FRANCIS, THE
EARLIER RULE,
1209/10–21

**The brutal sacking
of Constantinople
during the Fourth
Crusade, an
unforeseen turn
of events that left
Pope Innocent III
more powerful
than ever.**
*The Conquest of
Constantinople*
by Jacopo Palma.

F rancis knew that if he was going to attract 'many learned and noble men' to preach to 'kings and rulers and great crowds', then he and his men would have to become more than a local affair – a new order would need to be founded. If his Lord was going to 'multiply and increase his family throughout the entire world', he would need the approval of the church – more particularly, of the pope, Innocent III.

The mere thought of getting an audience with Pope Innocent III was ridiculous. Francis had sacrificed everything that would have made a positive impression on a man as sophisticated as Innocent, who, in a series of deft political and military moves, had become the most powerful man in Europe.

Innocent III had thwarted the Germans when they tried to wrest control of papal lands near Rome. The kings of Portugal, Aragon, Leon, Norway, Bohemia, Hungary and Bulgaria trembled at the political and moral pronouncements he directed at them. He subjected England to one of his interdicts, in which he denied the country the church's services and sacraments – and threatened King John with excommunication.

Then there was the oddity of the Fourth Crusade. Though sent off to recover Jerusalem, the Crusaders ended up sacking and pillaging the capital of Eastern Christendom, Constantinople. Innocent was appalled by the turn of events, but he ended up in control of the eastern half of the old Roman empire and the Eastern Orthodox Church.

Francis, the buoyant optimist, thought nothing impossible with God, and so he set off to Rome with his 11 companions. Francis insisted, as became his custom, that someone else lead the band for the journey, and Bernard was picked. The band stopped to pray frequently, and all along their journey they found people willing to give them food and shelter in the evenings.

St Peter's Basilica,
the church of the
popes. The
current edifice,
pictured here,
was completed
in 1615.

Arrival in Rome

When they arrived in Rome, they went immediately to the piazza in front of the Lateran, the epicentre of Europe's spiritual power. They passed the equestrian statue of the one whom everyone thought was the first great friend of the church, Emperor Constantine (later historians concluded that it was actually of Marcus Aurelius, one of the church's earliest persecutors). To the left was the pope's palace, next to it was the city's first basilica, and on the right was an eight-sided baptistry. The brothers headed

straight for the basilica, with its paintings, mosaics (notably that of Christ the redeemer) and the altar that everyone said contained relics of a table on which St Peter had said Mass.

They then walked to the *logia* of the palace, past ancient bronze statues (among them, that of the founders of ancient Rome, Romulus and Remus, sucking from a she-wolf). Then

providence or God smiled upon them again. They ran into
Bishop Guido of Assisi.

The bishop was just as surprised as the brothers, but
also perplexed. God forbid that Francis and his band were
leaving Assisi. The bishop thought of them as spiritual
assets to his diocese. He was relieved when he heard the
reason for their visit. He then introduced them to a good
friend, the cardinal bishop of Sabina, Lord John of St Paul.
It was more than a fortunate contact.

The cardinal, a Roman aristocrat by birth, had risen in

Church versus state

The rule of Innocent III shows how the church fought
morally and politically to control medieval society.
Innocent was born Lotario di Segni, and ascended
the throne of St Peter in 1198, at the age of 37. He
immediately began extending the church's control
over both secular and ecclesiastical spheres. First,
Innocent gained power in Italy, wresting control
from German princes, such as Count Conrad in Assisi.
When the German emperor Henry IV died, and two
aspirants (Otto IV and Philip of Swabia) vied for the
throne, Innocent threw his weight first behind one
and then behind the other, all the while asserting that
although 'the German princes have the right to elect
their king, who is afterwards to become emperor…
The right to investigate and decide a king thus elected
is worthy of imperial dignity belongs to the pope.'

Innocent strove to end hostilities between
Christian princes and placed interdicts against any,
such as Philip Augustus of France and Richard of
England, who refused to put down their arms. He declared the Magna Carta
null and void, mainly because it had been obtained by violence. He annulled
royal marriages in Portugal, settled succession disputes in Norway and Hungary,
and prepared crusades against Moors in Spain and heretics in France. Power for
Innocent III and most medieval popes, then, was mostly a means of asserting
what they felt was Christ's rightful sovereignty over the whole world.

the Curia on the strength of his learning, spirituality and wisdom. He was not only Innocent's confessor; his special expertise was knowing the difference between theological idiosyncrasy and heresy.

The cardinal was immediately sympathetic to Francis. He himself had financed a hospital near the Vatican. Though he was responsible for maintaining tight control of public spending in Rome, he gave generously to the poor. After several days of questioning Francis, he agreed to represent him to the pope.

'I have found a most perfect man, who wishes to live according to the form of the holy gospel, and to observe

A medieval 'map' of Rome, highlighting the holy places that pilgrims visited, by the Limburg brothers (c. 1415/16).

Church government

The Roman Catholic Church of the Middle Ages had become, in effect, another state on the European scene. The pope as head oversaw the Curia, a cabinet of cardinals, made up of archbishops, bishops, priests and deacons. The three main 'cabinet departments' were responsible for liturgy, correspondence and finances. Other cardinals oversaw matters of canon law, other still acted as the pope's legates on diplomatic missions. The pope even hired armies to wage war against sovereigns, such as Frederick II, who threatened papal lands.

evangelical perfection in all things,' he told Innocent and a group of cardinals. 'I believe that the Lord wills, through him, to reform the faith of the holy church throughout the world.'

This was no easy speech to make to this audience. Most of the cardinals did not appreciate Francis's implicit challenge to their luxurious lifestyle. A few of them had suffered the outrages of heretics, such as the Cathari, and they were in no mood to entertain a 'new teaching'. Nonetheless, Innocent asked to see Francis the next day.

Audience with the pope

Francis and his companions were escorted through the Lateran Palace, past the elegant dining hall, through the immense conference chamber and into the Hall of Mirrors. The 12 simple men in brown tunics found themselves facing the pope, judges and cardinals in caps or mitres, and robes of white, crimson or gold.

The contrast was in one way deceptive. Francis and Innocent III had a great deal in common. Both were musically inclined, had attractive voices and were capable of eloquence. They both had a sense of humour, as well. Innocent once joked that he regretted that his bishops were not always able to preach 'due to the surplus of their burdens, not to mention the deficit of their learning'.

Innocent was passionate about church reform and

'Francis's filial
love for the
Church of Rome
remains one
of the most
striking aspects
of his character.
From his youth
to the day he
died, his fidelity
to it never
wavered.'

JULIAN GREEN,
GOD'S FOOL, 1985

haunted by the possible demise of the church. Before Francis arrived, he had dreamed that the papal palace was on the verge of collapse, only held up by a small and shabbily dressed monk. This may have been a recurring dream; some said he had a similar dream during a visit of Dominic, the other great medieval reformer, years later.

As Francis pleaded his case for his new order, Innocent warmed to him. But he still had his doubts.

'My dear young sons, your life seems to us exceptionally hard and severe,' he finally replied. 'While we believe there can be no question about your living it because of your great zeal, we must take into consideration those who will come after you, lest this way of life seem too burdensome.'

Cardinal John of St Paul reminded the pope and the

What did Francis look like?

Several 13th-century painters drew portraits of Francis, and many historians think that the portrait by Cimabue in the lower church of the Basilica San Francesco (Church of St Francis) in Assisi is likely to be the most faithful. He painted it sometime about 1265, just a few decades after Francis's death. Many who knew Francis would have still been alive to confirm the likeness. It also corresponds to the description given by Thomas of Celano, one of Francis's earliest biographers, in *The Life of St Francis*:

He was of medium height, closer to short [his skeletal remains confirm that he would have stood 160 centimetres tall]; his head was of medium size and round. His face was somewhat long and drawn, his forehead small and smooth, with medium eyes black and clear. His hair was dark; his eyebrows straight, and his nose even and thin; his ears small and upright, and his temples smooth… His teeth were white [a feature that those who exhumed his remains briefly in 1978 especially noted], well set and even, his lips were small and thin; his beard black and sparse; his neck was slender, his shoulders straight; his arms were short, his hands slight, his fingers long and his nails tapered. He had thin legs, small feet, fine skin and little flesh.

cardinals, 'If we refuse the request of this poor man as novel or too difficult, when all he asks is to be allowed to lead the gospel life, we must be on our guard lest we commit an offence against Christ's gospel.'

He noted ironically that if anyone in the room was to argue that Francis's ideas were irrational or impossible, he would be saying that Christ's teaching on poverty were the same and would thus be 'guilty of blasphemy against Christ'.

But Innocent remained sceptical: 'My son, pray to Christ that through you he may show us his will, so that once we know it with more certainty, we may confidently approve your holy desire.'

So Francis and his companions took the next few days to pray. They attended Mass each day at one of the four principal basilicas in the city: St John Lateran, St Peter's, St Paul's (outside the walls) and Santa Maria Maggiore, dedicated to Christ's mother. While in prayer, or asleep one night, Francis had another of his visions. He described it to Innocent the next time they met:

There was a little, poor and beautiful woman in the desert, whose beauty fascinated a great king. He wanted to take her as his wife, because he thought that from her, he would have handsome sons. After the marriage was celebrated and consummated, there were many sons born and raised.

Their mother spoke to them in this way: 'My sons, do not be ashamed, for you are sons of the king. Therefore, go to his court and he will provide for all your needs.'

When they went to see the king, he was struck by their good looks, and noticing a resemblance to himself in them, he asked them, 'Whose sons are you?'

When they answered they were the sons of the little poor woman living in the desert, the king embraced them with great joy. 'Do not be afraid,' he said, 'for you are my sons. If strangers are fed at my table, how much more will you, who are my lawful sons.'

He then ordered the woman to send to his court all the children she had borne to be fed.

Francis then explained to the pope, 'My lord, I am that little woman whom the loving Lord, in his mercy, has adorned, and through whom he has been pleased to give birth to legitimate sons. The King of kings had told me he will nourish all the sons born to me, because, if he feeds strangers, he must provide for his own.'

To this appeal, Francis added a number of assurances. In contrast to the reform movements that gave the Curia headaches, he would not teach new doctrine nor denigrate the church's sacraments. He would also respect clergy and bishops. The pope still hesitated, but he did give informal approval for Francis to live his life and 'preach penance to everyone'. He did not wish to commit too much to the enterprise – nothing, for example, was put down in writing – but he did invite Francis to return in a few years: 'When almighty God increases you in number and grace, come back to us; we will grant you more and entrust you with greater charge.'

The pope also required Francis to be ordained a deacon, entitling him to read the Gospels in church (though not to administer the sacraments). In addition, the pope required that Francis and his companions, like all religious, be tonsured, meaning that the crown of the head would be shaved at least once a month.

With that, Francis's new order headed back to Assisi, intent on changing the world. As they journeyed back, Francis came to understand another mysterious dream he had had during the trip. In it, a strong, thick tree towered above him. As he marvelled at its height and beauty, suddenly he himself grew immense, to the very height of the tree. When he touched it, the tree bent easily to the ground. Francis, with a mixture of satisfaction and pride, noted that the great and towering tree of

Pope Innocent III prophetically dreamed that a crumbling church was supported by Francis. (Some stories say it was St Dominic.) *The Dream of Pope Innocent III* by Giotto di Bondone.

**The Basilica of
St Mary Major,
dating from the
fourth century,
is the largest
church dedicated
to Francis's
favourite saint.**

the papacy had indeed bent to his wishes. He had become more powerful than any knight.

When the party returned, they made Rivo Torto ('crooked stream') their new home, about one and a half kilometres from the Portiuncula. They passed the autumn and winter of 1209 in an abandoned hut, barely large enough to hold them all. Francis had to write their names on the beams to mark each brother's place to pray and sleep.

Life was not easy. 'The place was so cramped that they could barely sit or rest,' says *The Legend of the Three*

Companions. Sometimes their only meal was composed of the turnips they had begged for.

Yet, in *The Life of St Francis*, Thomas of Celano says that 'they… hardly ever stopped praying or praising God'. When they started to doze in prayer, they would prop themselves up with a stick to keep themselves awake. Some anchored themselves to the floor with ropes, so they would not toss and turn at night and disturb their neighbour who might be praying.

They were hardly perfect, however. Sometimes they ate or drank more than they believed was right. Sometimes fatigue tempted them away from their disciplines. Then remorse would set in, and they would punish their bodies to obey their highest desires.

They kept a holy silence most of the day, hardly speaking to one another; they did not want to be accused of idle chatter. They kept their gazes fixed to the ground so they would not be distracted from prayer by those around them.

Francis spoke with each of them daily about their spiritual state and, says Thomas, 'drove from their hearts any negligence'. He also examined himself, 'watchful of his guard at every hour'. And if any temptation struck him, Francis immediately plunged himself into a ditch filled with ice water, remaining in it until 'every seduction of the flesh went away'.

Then one day a peasant barged into the hut, pushing his donkey ahead of him, saying, 'Go in, go in, because we will do well in this place.' An annoyed Francis turned to his brothers and said, 'I know, brothers, that God did not call us to prepare a lodging for a donkey, nor to have dealings with men.' With that, Francis and his brothers left. They stayed a short time with some lepers before getting permission from the Benedictines to use the Portiuncula as their home.

'Francis, above all, seemed [at Rivo Torto] to be filled with a new ardour, and, like a valiant knight, he burned to throw himself into the thick of the fray.'

PAUL SABATIER,
*LIFE OF ST FRANCIS
OF ASSISI*, 1905

CHAPTER 6

The Earlier Rule

O ver the next dozen years, Francis's order exploded
in both numbers and geography. Twelve brothers
living together outside of Assisi became an order,
commonly called the Franciscans, whose thousands of
members could be found from England to Africa, from
Portugal to Hungary. This rapid growth left none of the
brothers time to chronicle events in these years. Because
of this, many incidents in the early biographies pile one
on top of the other, eluding historians' ability to pin them
down as to date or even sequence.

Even the Rule informally approved by the pope was
under constant revision during these years. It was an
informal guide when they left the pope's presence in
1209, but a formal document by Pentecost in 1221, when
it took the official form we now call the Earlier Rule.

In spite of some historical riddles, a close look at the
Earlier Rule (or the Rule, for the remainder of this chapter)
reveals the essence of Francis's vision. It also hints at what
it was that inspired men, and soon women, all across Europe
to cast in their lots with his seemingly strange regimen.

Obedience

The Rule says, 'The rule and life of these brothers
is this: namely to live in obedience, in chastity, and
without anything of their own, and to follow teaching
and footprints of our Lord Jesus Christ.' Though Francis
would become famous as a champion of poverty, the vow
of obedience came first for him.

Obedience was first for the brothers as well as for
Francis himself, as the Rule says: 'Brother Francis – and
whoever is head of this religion [that is, religious order]
– promises obedience and reverence to the Lord Pope

Innocent and his successors.' But it applied to all: 'Let all the brothers be bound to obey Brother Francis and his successors.' So important was obedience that the Franciscan life itself is sometimes summed up in this one word, for example, when the Rule speaks of new members being 'received into obedience'.

This was not a mindless obedience: 'If any one of the ministers [a brother in authority] commands one of the brothers something contrary to our life or his soul, he is not bound to obey him because obedience is not something in which a fault or sin is committed.' But other than that exception, Francis expected prompt obedience on all occasions: 'Carry out an order at once,' he told the brothers, 'and don't wait for it to be repeated. Don't plead or object that anything in a command is impossible.'

On this point, Francis often became exasperated with his brothers. One day he blurted out, 'There is hardly a single religious in the whole world who obeys his superior well!'

The brothers with him were alarmed, and they asked, 'Tell us, Father, what is the perfect and best form of obedience?'

'Take up a dead body', he replied, 'and lay it where you will. You will see that it does not resist being moved, or complain… or ask to be left alone!'

Obedience for Francis was the foundation of humility, the cardinal virtue of a Franciscan brother. Thus, whenever Francis embarked on a trip, he always appointed another brother to be in charge so that he, Francis, could practise obedience as well. Francis abolished the title of 'prior' and settled on 'minister' or even 'servant' for those in authority in the order. And the brothers, no matter their title, were to wash one another's feet, and if a brother hurt or provoked another, he must kiss the foot of the offended brother in apology.

Obedience was not passive or something a superior could demand autocratically, but something the brothers offered one another as a gift: 'Let no brother do or say anything evil to another; on the contrary, through the charity of the Spirit, let them serve and obey one another voluntarily. This is the true and holy obedience of our Lord Jesus Christ.'

Along with submission came another duty: the brothers held each other and their superiors accountable. They were to admonish them 'if they see any of them walking according to the flesh and not

Francis and his first 12 disciples receive Innocent III's blessing on their way of life. (Some historians say that only 11 disciples accompanied Francis, making a total of 12). Fresco by Giotto di Bondone in the Bardi chapel, Santa Croce, Florence.

according to the Spirit in keeping with the integrity of our life'.

Watching out for each other's sins, Francis recognized, could easily tempt the brothers to self-righteousness. Thus, the Rule added that both ministers and brothers should 'be careful not to be disturbed or angered at another's sin or evil, because the devil wishes to destroy many because of another's fault'. Monitoring another's spiritual life was to be an act of concern so that all would grow in spiritual maturity. It was not to be a game of 'Gotcha!'

Furthermore, Francis encouraged his brothers to go to one another for help and guidance: 'Let each one confidently make known his need to another that the other might discover what is needed and minister to him.' This rule may have arisen because the early brothers were striving heroically, but often silently, about their spiritual struggles. But, as Francis reminded the brothers, they should be able to count on one another's compassion: 'Let each one love and care for his brother as a mother loves and cares for her son in those matters in which God has given him grace.'

Francis illustrated this early on, while the brothers were still at Rivo Torto. They were in the middle of a particularly severe fast when, one night around midnight, one of the brothers cried out, 'I'm dying! I'm dying!' The other brothers woke up, startled and frightened.

'Brothers, get up and light a lamp,' ordered Francis. When the lamp was lit, he asked, 'Who was it who said, "I'm dying"?'

Francis (in the circle) miraculously appears in a vision to Franciscans gathered at Arles, France. Altar panel attributed to Bonaventura Berlinghieri in the Bardi chapel, Santa Croce, Florence.

After the brother, probably sheepishly, identified himself, Francis asked, 'What's the matter, brother? Why are you dying?'

'I'm dying of hunger,' he said.

Francis immediately ordered that the table be set, and they all ate a meal together with the brother. When they were done eating, Francis said, 'My brothers, I say that each of you must consider his own constitution, because, although one of you may be sustained with less food than another, I still do not want one who needs more food to try imitating him in this… Just as we must beware of overindulgence in eating, which harms body and soul, so we must beware of excessive abstinence even more, because the Lord desires mercy not sacrifice.'

Francis tempered his demand for obedience, then, with mercy.

Worship and work

In popular imagination, Francis and his brothers were carefree nature lovers who wandered the countryside picking flowers, singing with the birds and composing poems extolling the wonders of nature. The brothers actually had little time for such frivolities, as they would call them. Rather than selfishly basking in a sunny meadow, they went about giving themselves completely to God and to others.

They conceived of their main work as prayer, and not a spontaneous, carefree prayer, but the regular prayers prescribed by the church: 'Let all the brothers, whether clerical or lay, recite the Divine Office, the praises and prayers, as is required of them,' says the Rule. This liturgy, also called the Daily Office, consisted of seven services of prayer each day (known as the Hours), called Matins, Prime, Terce, Sext, None, Vespers and Compline. In addition to the church's requirements for these services, Francis added his own: 'Let the lay brothers say the [Apostles'] Creed and 24 Our Fathers with the Glory to the Father for Matins… for Prime, the Creed and seven Our Fathers with the Glory to the Father…' and so on for each service. In addition, the brothers read Bible passages in each service, so that all 150 Psalms were said each week and the entire Bible was read every 12 months.

Francis composed prayers of his own for each of the services, in a cycle sometimes called *The Office of the Passion*. He had the brothers not only read, but also memorize these.

These formal prayers did not result in a merely formal relationship with the divine. The brothers experienced many moments of mystical rapture. One night, while Francis was away praying in the Assisi cathedral, one of the brothers, who himself was praying alone late into the night, suddenly saw a chariot sweeping back and forth around the rafters of their small hut. He watched in amazement, and then woke the brothers, who said they also saw it. They all interpreted it to be the soul of Francis at prayer.

Another time, Bishop Guido made a call on Francis while Francis prayed in his cell. When Bishop Guido tried to open the cell door and stick his head inside, he was met by an inexplicable force: 'All of a sudden,' says *The Assisi Compilation*, an early collection of stories about Francis, 'by the will of the Lord… he was forcefully pushed outside, willy-nilly, stumbling backwards.' The brothers chalked it up to be the spiritual force of Francis's prayer life.

It is hard to know how to take such stories, since they border on the mythical. In any event, they are not central to Franciscan spirituality. Francis never told his brothers to seek mystical moments and, as much as he exalted prayer, he wanted more than prayer from the brothers:

Dominic with some of his friers.
Scene from the Life of St Dominic (Italian, early 14th century).

Dominic's new order

Francis was not the only visionary who was trying to change the world by founding a new order. Another was Dominic (1170–1221).

When he was Bishop Domingo de Guzman, Dominic took a mission through southern France to convert the Cathari in Languedoc. On this trip, the bishop was shocked to meet members of the Cistercian Order who, in also trying to convert the ascetic Cathari, were trying to impress them with their horses, regalia, fancy robes and fine food. 'The heretics are to be converted by an example of humility… far more readily than by any external display or verbal battles,' he said. 'So let us arm ourselves with devout prayers and set off showing signs of genuine humility and barefooted to combat Goliath.'

This was the germ idea from which the Dominican Order eventually emerged. Besides embracing poverty, the Blackfriars (as they came to be known, from the colour of their cloaks), specialized in preaching and teaching to refute heretical arguments. With papal approval in 1215, their official name became the Order of Preachers.

This twofold approach of humility and persuasiveness convinced many a heretic to convert – but not enough, apparently. The Dominicans eventually agreed with the papacy that the church could defeat heresy only if it also applied political and social pressure as well, so they became key players in the Inquisition in the coming centuries.

After Dominic's death and subsequent canonization (1234), the order continued to grow rapidly, counting 12,000 followers within a century. They attracted not only the great souls of the era, such as the mystic Catherine of Siena, but also the greatest minds, such as that of Thomas Aquinas. Together with the Franciscans, says historian Adrian House in *Francis of Assisi: A Revolutionary Life*, they were 'the most distinctive and original force for good in medieval Europe'.

'Let them [the brothers] be careful not to appear outwardly as sad and gloomy hypocrites but show themselves joyful, cheerful, and consistently gracious in the Lord.'

FRANCIS, THE
EARLIER RULE,
1209/10–21

'Francis was not a systematic theologian articulating an explicit, developed doctrine of poverty. He preferred acting out the truth to stating it in bald words.'

WILLIAM S.
STAFFORD, VIRGINIA
THEOLOGICAL
SEMINARY,
CHRISTIAN HISTORY
MAGAZINE, 1994

'Let all the brothers always strive to exert themselves in doing good works, for it is written, "Always do something good that the devil may find you occupied."' And again, '"Idleness is an enemy of the soul." Servants of God, therefore, must always apply themselves to prayer or some good work.' Thus, we find the brothers, when not in prayer or worship, visiting lepers, planting, threshing, nursing families with smallpox or dysentery and so on.

Poverty

The incident when the man and donkey burst into the brothers' hut at Rivo Torto may have been the occasion for Francis's penning of another key sentence in his Rule: 'Wherever the brothers may be, either in hermitages or other places, let them be careful not to make any place their own or contend with anyone for it. Whoever comes to them, friend or foe, thief or robber, let him be received with kindness.'

Francis is famous for embracing poverty at any cost, and rightly so. It went hand in hand with the humility that Francis wanted to instil in himself and his brothers. It was also a way of transforming a world that seemed to know only the rule of acquisition at any cost.

In a hermitage north of Borgo San Sepulcro, some thieves would regularly come and ask the brothers

Previous pages:
There are
multiple stories
of Francis giving
up his cloak to
others more in
need, and in
some cases
(not shown here),
Francis was
left naked.
*St Francis Gives
His Cloak to a
Poor Knight* by
Giotto di
Bondone.

for bread. The brothers knew very well who these men were because their reputation for highway robbery was widespread. Soon, the brothers began to question their generosity: 'It's wrong to give them alms,' they reasoned, 'for they are robbers who inflict all sorts of evil on people.' When Francis made one of his regular visits to them, they asked him what they should do.

Francis, as usual, turned the tables on them. He told them not to wait for the thieves to come to them, but to prepare a meal, then go to find the robbers and invite them to eat: 'Spread out a tablecloth on the ground, put the bread and wine on it, and serve them with humility and good humour.' Once the robbers were in a good mood, they were to ask them one favour: 'Make them promise you not to strike any man and not to harm anyone.'

After that, Francis told them to prepare another meal, and then another and so on. At each meal, the brothers were to ask the robbers to give up one more piece of their trade. The story goes that the robbers slowly gave up their ways and converted to Francis's order.

Such generosity arose from their complete freedom from possessions. Not only did the brothers relinquish all

On loan from on high

Something of Francis's reasoning about possessions comes through in one story told by Thomas of Celano. Francis was returning from Siena with a companion when a poor man, barely clothed, approached them. 'Brother,' Francis said to his companion, 'we must give back to this poor man the mantle that is his. We accepted it on loan until we should happen to find someone poorer than we are.'

The companion vehemently disagreed, saying that Francis should not expose himself to the elements to help this poor man. But Francis would have none of it, and ended up giving away his mantle. Francis thought that everything he possessed was merely on loan from God and, as such, he needed to give it away if another had more need of it than he did.

rights to individual ownership of any item, the Rule forbade the order itself from owning land or buildings. Wherever they lived or stayed, they depended on the invitation and hospitality – and whims – of others. If it was not hard enough to conceive of sustaining a growing order with this restriction, Francis added one more: 'Let none of the brothers... wherever he may be or go, carry, receive, or have received in any way coin or money, whether for clothing, books, or payment for work.'

If a brother was sick, or a leper needed immediate medical attention, Francis permitted begging for money to pay for a doctor or medicine. But other than that, the brothers were never to touch money. They were not even to be seen with a beggar who asked for money.

Francis saved some of his strongest language for offenders of this rule: 'If by chance, God forbid, it happens that some brother is collecting or holding coin or money... let all the brothers consider him a deceptive brother, an apostate, a thief, a robber.'

He also saved some of his harshest disciplines for those who broke this rule. According to *The Assisi Compilation*, one day a layman happened to enter St Mary of the Angels to pray and, as an offering, he laid some money near the cross. After he left, a brother unthinkingly picked the money up and placed it on a window ledge. When the brother heard that Francis had learned of the incident, he immediately rushed to Francis and implored his forgiveness. He even offered his body, saying Francis should whip him for penance. Francis, however, was not so easily placated; he had a better idea. After rebuking the brother sternly, he ordered him to go to the window sill, pick up the money with his mouth and carry it outside. Then, again with his mouth, he was to deposit it on a heap of ass's dung. The brother obeyed gladly.

Francis believed that money was like a drug, as addictive and destructive to the soul as we today believe heroin or cocaine are to the body. For Francis, money was not something one could use moderately or 'recreationally' without it eventually enslaving the soul. He took literally Jesus' statement that one cannot serve God and mammon, as well as the command to give away one's coat if asked for it.

Stories of Francis giving things away, especially his mantle, abound in the early biographies. One winter's day, an old woman approached Francis and his companion while they were staying at the bishop's palace in Celano. She asked for alms, but Francis merely took the cloth that was wrapped around his neck to keep him warm and gave it to her, saying, 'Go and make yourself a tunic; you really need it.' The old woman thought it was a joke and laughed. But when Francis just stood there extending the wrap to her, she suddenly grabbed it and ran off. As she was cutting it up to make it into a tunic, she soon realized that she would be short of cloth. So she returned to Francis and told him of her problem. Francis then turned to his companion and said, 'Brother, do you hear what this old woman is saying? For the love of God, let us bear with the cold!' With that, Francis and the brother gave the woman their cloaks, and both of them were left standing in their underwear.

Chastity

Chastity was, of course, another cardinal feature of the brothers' life, as it had been of all the orders of the Roman Catholic Church for 1,000 years. But Francis was after more than formal chastity. Again, the ultimate goal was freedom – in this case, freedom from a passion that, as much as any other, has the ability to consume and distract people from more virtuous pursuits.

So the brothers worked at this long before they ever put themselves in a position to physically break their vows: 'Wherever they may be or may go, let all the brothers avoid evil glances and associations with women. No one may counsel them, travel alone with them or eat out of the same dish with them.' This was not because women were evil but because, human nature being what it is, one thing leads to another. If one wants complete freedom in anything, it is best to begin at the source.

However, as the history of asceticism shows, this freedom is hard to win, and Francis's brothers found it no easier than have aspirants of any era. At Rivo Torto, for example, while the brothers experienced extraordinary moments of mystical elation, lust remained a frequent and disturbing temptation. Their regular antidote was to jump into a ditch of icy water in winter, or scourge themselves in summer – the medieval version of the cold shower.

Francis's temptations

Francis readily admitted that he was tempted by the very things he warned his brothers about.

As his notoriety increased, Francis tried to keep his humility and wits about him. When people tried to touch his garments in veneration, he told them not to canonize him too soon, adding that a 'saint' such as him might still fall into temptation, and 'bring sons and daughters into this world'.

In spite of his spiritual advancements – and maybe because of them – he still found himself battling against what Thomas of Celano, in *The Remembrance of the Desire of a Soul*, called 'a violent temptation to lust'. One winter's day, while he prayed at a hillside hermitage at Sarteano, he suffered an especially severe bout. So he took off all his clothes, and 'lashed himself furiously' with a whip; he addressed his body as 'Brother Ass' and scolded it for its lustful passions.

When that seemed to have no effect, he went out to the garden and threw himself naked onto the snow. He then made seven snowmen, and went on to lecture himself: 'Here, this large one is your wife, and those four over there are your two sons and your two daughters; the other two are your servant and your maid, who are needed to serve them. So hurry, get all of them some clothes, because they're freezing to death! But if complicated care of them is annoying, then take care to serve one Master!'

Catholics through and through

'Let all the brothers live and speak as Catholics,' says the
Rule. Faithfulness to things Catholic was the decisive test
of loyalty for Francis: 'If someone has strayed in word or
in deed from Catholic faith and life and has not amended
his way, let him be expelled from our brotherhood.'

It was not just a matter of loyalty and respect, but of
obedience to something larger than themselves: 'Let us

Franciscan monks
at service.
Illustration from
Richard II's psalter.

consider all clerics and religious as our masters in all that pertains to the salvation of our soul and does not deviate from our religion.' This was not merely politic – a way of fending off charges of heresy or schism. More than anything, it was another means of instilling humility.

Francis was not blind. He did not fail to see the rank corruption that infected the church, high and low. He was, after all, on a mission to reform the church. He knew that the priests had concubines, that bishops greedily accumulated land, that archbishops lived lives of luxury and that popes loved power. Still, he told his brothers that when they met a priest, no matter his reputation, they were to bow and kiss his hand, and if he was mounted, they were also to kiss the hooves of his horse. For one, priests administered the eucharist, which brought Christ tangibly to the people. For another, any reasonable person could honour those who deserve honour. But only a humble person could do what Francis asked of his brothers.

'If they obstruct the salvation of the people,' he explained, 'vengeance belongs to God, and he will punish them in his own time… If you are sons of peace, you will win both clergy and people, and this will be more pleasing to God than if you were to win the people alone and alienate the clergy. Conceal their mistakes and make up for their many defects; and when you have done this, be even more humble than before.'

From start to finish, then, the Rule nourished humility. But it was not humility for humility's sake. Humility was the highest virtue for Francis because, more than any other virtue, it prepared the soul to receive and praise God.

The Rule was a tool designed to quash any human affection that stood in the way of God. This is why Francis said, 'Let us hate our body with its vices and sins, because by living in the flesh, the

'Let everyone be struck with fear, let the whole world tremble, and let the heavens exult when Christ, the Son of the living God, is present on the altar in the hands of a priest!'

FRANCIS, *A LETTER TO THE ENTIRE ORDER*, 1225–26

devil wishes to take away from us the love of Jesus Christ and eternal life.' Talk of 'hating the body' was common in the Middle Ages, and it unfortunately encouraged a great deal of self-abuse: people whipping themselves, fasting excessively and so on. Even Francis was guilty of this, and his own bodily abuse led to his relatively early death at the age of 46. But what the medieval world grasped rightly in all this was the truth that the body, with its ravenous desires for food, sleep, leisure and sex, often undermines complete devotion to God.

To be fair, Francis and most medieval spiritual counsellors were not dualists. The body needed discipline, yes, but it was not itself the source of evil. Quoting freely from Jesus, Francis wrote in the Rule, 'From the heart proceed and come evil thoughts, adultery, fornication, murder, theft, greed, malice, deceit, licentiousness, envy, false witness, blasphemy, foolishness.' He concluded, 'All these evils come from within a person's heart, and these are what defile a person.'

Obedience, poverty, chastity, prayer, loyalty and all the rest were means by which his brothers could atone for their defilement, conquer temptation and give themselves completely to God. At the end of the Rule, Francis appended an extended, poetic exhortation that sums up what every line of the Rule is about:

Therefore,
  let us desire nothing else,
  let us want nothing else,
  let nothing else please us and cause us delight except our
    Creator, Redeemer, and Saviour,
  the only true God,
Who is the fullness of good,
  All good, every good, the true and supreme good,
Who alone is good,
  Merciful, gentle, delightful, and sweet,
Who alone is holy,
  Just, true, holy, and upright,

Who alone is kind, innocent, clean,
   From whom, through whom, and in whom
   Is all pardon, all grace, all glory
Of all penitents and just ones,
   Of all the blessed rejoicing together in heaven.

C H A P T E R   7

Clare

O nce people began to believe that Francis had a special relationship with God, the order began to grow. It was not so unusual any more for men of some standing to seek Francis out. Young men such as Masseo di Massignano, who came from one of the better families in the area, was one example. He was proverbially tall, dark and handsome, and a dynamic public speaker as well. He also had the necessary arrogance found in every successful politician, which is why everyone said that his political future looked bright. Instead, he decided that success meant a life of humility and poverty in obedience to Francis.

A second convert, Rufino di Scipione came from one of Assisi's most powerful and controversial families. He had joined the order after watching a violent quarrel between two Franciscan brothers. (This is evidence that Francis's brothers were, in spite of their discipline and piety, still very human.) Just as the two were about to come to blows, Brother Barbaro, who had been the more aggressive, suddenly bent down, grabbed some dung lying on the ground and shoved it into his mouth. This symbolized what he thought of the harsh words that had spewed from his own mouth. He then apologized to his companion. This act of humility won over Rufino immediately.

A third key recruit at this time was Leo, a priest from Assisi. He soon became Francis's confessor, secretary and almost constant companion. (Later, Leo joined Rufino and Angelo [Francis's 12th recruit] in writing two documents – *The Assisi Compilation* and *The Legend of the Three Companions* – which give us valuable information about Francis.) But it was not just men who were drawn to Francis during these exciting years.

Not everyone taken with Francis could abandon family and vocation to follow him. So Francis, recognizing their situation, outlined in his document *A Letter to the Faithful* how they might live. This became the basis for the Rule of the Third Order, which Cardinal Ugolino approved in 1221.

Tertiaries, as they were called, were to dress modestly, and to avoid banquets and dances. They were to eat but two meals a day and to fast every Friday (and some Wednesdays). They were each to give away 10 per cent of their income, pay off their debts and make restitution for any goods they had unjustly gained. They were to observe all the hours of the daily office and, if they could not, they were to say 54 'Our Fathers' and 'Glory Be to the Fathers'. They were supposed to examine their consciences every night, confess their sins and receive the eucharist three times a year. Once a month, they were to meet with other tertiaries to worship together.

Three features, in particular, made the Third Order a potent force for social change. First, tertiaries were to will their estate to the poor or to the church. This created a significant social welfare system. Second, they were forbidden from carrying arms. This cut down on the incessant violence of the era. Third, they were only permitted to makes oaths to God or to the pope. This freed the tertiary from many feudal obligations, for since he had given his allegiance to the pope, he was now subject not to secular courts, but to church courts. The popes used this allegiance to thwart the aggression of the Holy Roman Empire; instead of serving the emperor in battle, the tertiaries could serve the Church. Overall, this vow helped to bring more peace to an era characterized by incessant 'gang warfare'.

We do not know the numbers of men and women who committed themselves to the Third Order, but the order has had among its ranks some of history's most influential people, including many popes, King Louis IX (St Louis), Michelangelo and Christopher Columbus.

A female follower

Given the station that she had been born into, Clare di Favarone should have lived a peaceful and sheltered life. As it turned out, the best known of Francis's female disciples grew up knowing violence and terror. As a child, she lived with her parents and sisters in a *palazzo* they shared with the rest of their extended family on the San Rufino Piazza. She was four years old when angry Assisians destroyed

Duke Conrad's castle and then, one by one, began attacking the homes of Assisi's wealthy and powerful people. Her family escaped to rival Perugia until things settled down.

Clare's father, Favarone di Offreduccio, was a knight. Her aristocratic mother, Ortolana, was a woman with a deep religious devotion. She made many pilgrimages to Rome, one to Mount Gargano on the Apulia coast (where Michael the Archangel was said to have visited) and one to Jerusalem – a journey considered dangerous even for a man. After she felt she had sufficiently atoned for her sins, she settled down with her husband and bore him Clare (in 1193 or 1194), then Catherine (in 1197) and finally Beatrice (in 1205).

Clare adopted her mother's piety early on. Clare's spiritual hero was the Roman martyr St Agnes, whose refusals to give up her virginity, no matter the cost, proved her devotion to Christ. The traditional story goes that Agnes' parents became so angry at her refusal to entertain suitors that they sent her to a brothel. But God protected Agnes's sexual modesty, growing her hair miraculously long so that her body could not be seen, and protecting her from the flames when she was put to the stake. It took a beheading to kill her, the legend says.

Clare said more than her share of prayers, dressed modestly, and saved food from her meals and gave them to her friend, Bona, to distribute to the needy. From time to time, she also asked Bona to take food to the Portiuncula, where her childhood friends Angelo and Rufino were members of the order that Francis Bernadone had started.

Most Assisians thought Francis a fanatic and, perhaps for that very reason, the 16-year-old Clare was curious. One Sunday, she went to hear him preach at the cathedral, and she was henceforth smitten with his devotion and passion. She wanted to know more, but she knew that her parents would forbid her from talking with the outcast. So, one evening, she sneaked off with her six-year-old sister Beatrice and Bona to meet secretly with Francis, then aged 29, and one of his friends. Soon enough, she felt a call to

Opposite page: The austere beauty of Clare, Francis's first and most famous female disciple, shines through this fresco detail from the lower church of Basilica San Francesco. Attributed to Simone Martini and others.

do something with her life that she knew her family would not approve of.

At about this time, Clare came into some money. Her father had died and left her dowry to her. The pressure on her to marry intensified – she was, after all, a good catch: well-educated (at home, anyway) and well-connected – a marriage that would bring many tangible benefits to the Offreduccios. But Clare managed to stall the suitors with whom her family set her up. When she turned 18, she announced that she was going to give away her money to the poor.

Her uncle Monaldo, the head of the family, was stunned. He pleaded with her to change her mind. So did a neighbour, Ranieri di Bernardo, who even proposed to her. Clare would have none of it.

Then, on the night of Palm Sunday in 1212, as her mother, uncles and cousins slept, Clare slipped silently down the stairs of the *palazzo*, turned away from the main door guarded by a man-at-arms, and quietly removed the pile of rocks and the heavy beams that blocked a back door. She forced it open and slipped away via a back lane. She met up with Pacifica, one of her mother's lifelong companions, and her cousin Rufino, who guided them to the Portiuncula.

Francis and a few companions were waiting with torches when Clare arrived. They escorted her into the church, where she made her confession and received absolution from Sylvester, a priest who now followed Francis. She took off the beautiful dress she had been wearing since morning services, and put on a simple habit. Then she made her vows ('I promised him obedience,' she wrote years later in her *Testament*). To seal the vows, Francis cut her pale, almost gold hair in the form of a tonsure.

Francis, Clare and all present rejoiced, but only for the moment. They were still in danger, so Clare was hurried off to nearby St Paul's (San Paulo), a Benedictine convent protected personally by the pope. Francis felt that

'Never was there a closer and more harmonious union than that existing between St Clare and St Francis. Never were two souls in more perfect accord in their way of looking at things of earth and heaven.'

OMAR ENGLEBERT,
*ST FRANCIS
OF ASSISI:
A BIOGRAPHY*, 1965

she would be safe there from any legal or physical assaults of her family. It turned out that Clare needed more than ecclesiastical protection.

Monaldo led seven Offreduccios by horseback to St Paul's and forced their way inside the convent. Monaldo demanded that Clare return home. She refused. This scenario was repeated several times over the next few days, with Monaldo alternating threats with bribes, all to no avail. One day, Monaldo and his party cornered Clare in a chapel and lunged at her. She grasped the altar as they tried to pull her away. Clare's head-covering fell to the floor, and they all gasped. The aggressors saw that she had been tonsured, that she had already taken the crucial symbolic step of a cloistered life. They abandoned their quest and went on their way.

A little later, Catherine, Clare's now 16-year-old sister, fled home and joined Clare, and Monaldo led a party of 11 men to rescue her. Again, he pleaded and threatened and, again, lost his patience. One of the knights rushed up to Catherine, and tried to slap and kick her into submission. He grabbed her hair while others tried to grab her flailing arms to carry her.

She was dragged down a hill and over a muddy path. Bushes tore at her clothes, and her hair came out in tufts as she fought. The story goes that, at just this moment, a helpless Clare, who had been witnessing the horrid scene, dropped to her knees in prayer. Suddenly, the armed guard – perhaps exhausted from the struggle, perhaps ashamed of having abused Catherine into near-unconsciousness, perhaps merely prompted by divine command – abandoned her.

In the early days, it was not easy becoming a Franciscan! At any rate, eventually the family left Clare and Catherine alone. In fact, Pacifica, the 40-year-old friend of Clare's mother, joined the girls and, later, so did Clare's sister Beatrice. Catherine eventually changed her name to Agnes, who was her hero as well. Francis arranged it so these women could stay permanently at San Damiano, and he gave them his official blessing and support in a brief letter to Clare: 'Since by divine inspiration you have made yourselves daughters and servants of the most high King, the heavenly Father, and have taken the Holy Spirit as your spouse, choosing to live according to the perfection of the holy gospel, I resolve and promise for myself and for my brothers always to have that same loving care and special solicitude for you as [I have] for them.'

The Poor Ladies

In this way, a new order was born. They called themselves the Poor Ladies (today they are known as the Poor Clares). Within a few years, Clare had 50 sisters at San Damiano, many of the women having come from the better families in the region.

Opposite page: Clare repels the armies of Frederick II with prayer and the blessed host – one of the best-known miracles attributed to her. Detail from *Tree of Life of the Franciscans*, a 15th-century Flemish tapestry.

Francis's brothers begged food for them, supplied them with firewood and built them extra rooms when their numbers expanded. The women dressed simply, worked with their hands (for example, producing altar linens for local churches), and prayed and fasted like the Franciscan brothers. Clare, like Francis, fasted so severely that she often became ill. When Francis heard of one bout of illness brought on by fasting, he ordered that, from then on, she was not to go for 24 hours without at least a little food.

Like the brothers, the sisters prayed together several times a day in the chapel, and gave regular confessions to Leo and Sylvester, who also celebrated Mass for them. Clare prayed even more hours, before the others had even risen for the day and after all had drifted off into sleep. The sister noted that she often cried as she meditated on the crucifixion of Christ. The slightest word could transport her into mystical ecstasy. One Sunday, she was so struck by one antiphon that she spent the rest of the day sprinkling her companions with holy water to remind them of the water that flowed from Jesus' side.

Clare insisted on calling the Poor Ladies sisters, rather than nuns, for she believed that they shared equally in the work and worship of the order. She was just 21 years old

Staving off an army

Many artists have depicted Clare's most legendary miracle, which many scholars conclude occurred on a Friday in September 1240. The imperial army, composed of mercenary Saracens that Frederick II had hired, had invaded central Italy, 'burning cities, cutting down trees, laying waste vineyards, and torturing women and children', according to the *Legend of St Clare* (1255). And they showed no restraint when they fought the pope's armies, and displayed even less respect for any nuns who fell into their hands.

Assisi found itself in the middle of this war and, on this Friday, some imperial soldiers began scaling the walls of San Damiano, intent on entering the cloister. In desperation, Clare grabbed the sacrament and marched towards the invaders, praying, 'Lord Jesus, do not permit these defenceless virgins to fall into the hands of these heathen. Protect them. For I, who have nourished them with your love, can do nothing for them.' She prayed like this for the city of Assisi as well.

'Immediately,' says the *Legend of St Clare*, 'the boldness of those dogs was changed into fear and they quickly clambered over the walls they had scaled.' This was one of the miracles described to authorities during Clare's canonization hearings.

'Place your
mind before the
mirror of
eternity! Place
your soul in the
brilliance of
glory! Place
your heart in
the figure
of divine
substance! And
transform your
whole being into
the image of the
Godhead itself
through
contemplation.'

CLARE OF ASSISI,
THIRD LETTER TO
AGNES OF PRAGUE
(1238)

when church authorities insisted that she accept the role of abbess in the community. She agreed reluctantly, but she never used the title during her 40 years of service.

Clare was as ascetically heroic as her mentor. To discipline her flesh, she slept on boards and, when she was not fasting, she refused to eat cooked food. (As she got older, she realized the need to temper such asceticism, as she wrote to her sister Agnes in 1229: 'Our flesh is not of bronze, nor is our strength that of stone. So I urge you to be less strenuous in your fasting, so as to render reasonable worship to the Lord.') Clare also fetched water for sisters who were too ill to get out of bed, and washed the mattresses of the sick ('not running away from their filth nor shrinking from their stench', says one account). She even washed and kissed the feet of her sisters as a sign of her respect.

As Clare's reputation for sanctity spread, so did the belief in her ability to perform cures and other miracles. Francis, for example, sent brother Stephen to her when he thought that Stephen was suffering from some form of madness. Clare made the sign of the cross over Stephen (as she did to everyone who came to her), and then told him to go to sleep in the place where she normally prayed. The story goes that the next morning, when he arose, he was in his right mind, and he returned to Francis immediately.

In spite of her good works and efficacious prayers, Clare could not get official recognition of her order. The sticking point for each papal administration was her wish that her order should not own property, but simply rent or live off the goodwill of those who did own property. For Clare, this went to the very heart of what she and Francis were about. The forsaking of possessions was required not only of individuals, but of the whole order.

Clare, like Francis, sought to emulate Jesus. In her *Testament*, written at the end of her life, she exhorted her sisters to always observe poverty: 'out of love of the God who was placed poor in the crib, lived poor in the world, and remained naked on the cross'. Physical poverty, however, was merely a means of attaining poverty of spirit, which was necessary to make room for Jesus within.

In this, she saw the Virgin Mary as the prime model. As she told Agnes, 'As the glorious Virgin of virgins carried him materially, so you, too, by following her footprints, especially those of poverty and humility, can without any doubt, always carry him spiritually in your chaste and virginal body, holding him by whom all things are held together.'

Papal officials who, in this case, seemed to understand human nature better than Clare, insisted that severe poverty and relinquishing ownership was unrealistic and would eventually sabotage the order. In 1218, when papal legate Cardinal Ugolino approved a rule for the Poor Sisters, it lacked the provision about forsaking ownership. Clare protested, but Ugolino would not budge. This tug of war over poverty continued for the rest of Clare's life. But on her deathbed, in August 1253, a messenger told her that the pope had approved her rule, which included the provision she had long fought for – the first approved rule written by a woman.

Clare and Francis

Clare's own achievements were many, and her relationship with Francis was one of the most spiritually intimate between a man and a woman. *The Little Flowers of St Francis*, a collection of stories about Francis edited some 100 years after his death, contains a story that best characterizes their relationship. Many stories in the book have the aura of legend about them and tend to overstress the miraculous. Yet they often are able to throw unexpected light on Francis. One story tells of a remarkable meal enjoyed by Francis and Clare.

Francis had often visited Clare at San Damiano to give her spiritual counsel but, for years, Clare had wanted to visit the Portiuncula, the home of her spiritual father, a

'O God-centred poverty, whom the Lord Jesus Christ, who ruled and now rules heaven and earth… condescended to embrace before all else.'

CLARE OF ASSISI,
FIRST LETTER TO
AGNES OF PRAGUE
(1234)

'What a great laudable exchange: to leave the things of time for those of eternity, to choose the things of heaven for the goods of earth, to receive the hundredfold in place of one, and to possess a blessed and eternal life.'

CLARE OF ASSISI,
FIRST LETTER TO
AGNES OF PRAGUE
(1234)

Transcendent friendship

Clare's uncompromising commitment to poverty and to Christ so impressed Francis that Clare soon became one of his most trusted confidants. Though he was Clare's religious superior, Francis deferred to Clare's judgment often when it came to making decisions for her community.

In his later years, he depended more and more on her care (when he fell ill) and advice. For one period, Francis debated about whether he should give up his life as an itinerant preacher and instead become a hermit, devoting his life completely to prayer. As he wrestled with this decision, he asked for prayer from only two people: his former confessor, Sylvester, and Clare. (Both advised him to remain an evangelist.) At the end of Francis's life, it was Clare who nursed him at San Damiano for weeks.

The stiff formality of this Renaissance illuminated initial of Francis and Clare attempts to tame the intimate and passionate spiritual relationship they were said to share.

Some modern biographers find it impossible to believe that Clare and Francis did not share some sort of romantic attraction, but this is to read a modern sensibility back into the medieval world, which had a larger imagination that does our own age. Even if their relationship was charged by subliminal sexual attraction, that energy was clearly channelled into something transcendent – a common commitment to incarnate the humility and poverty of Christ in their world.

place that, to her, was holy. After Francis had rejected her numerous requests (probably to keep female contact with his brothers to a minimum), she asked intermediaries to intercede for her.

'Father, we do not think this rigidity is in keeping with divine love,' they began. They reminded Francis that Clare's request for a simple meal was a small favour, especially considering how 'holy and beloved' Clare was. Do not forget, they added, 'it was through your preaching that she abandoned the world and her riches'.

After going back and forth, Francis finally relented. 'If it seems good to you, it seems good to me.' He concluded that Clare, who indeed had been cloistered for many years at San Damiano, should 'see again the place where her hair was cut and where she became a bride of Christ'.

The day arrived, and Clare, escorted by one of her sisters and some Franciscan brothers, arrived. She reverently greeted the statue of the Virgin, where she had received the veil, and then was given a tour of the place.

Meanwhile, Francis had prepared a meal and spread it on the bare ground, as was his custom. Clare, some sisters, Francis and a few brothers sat down. Francis began speaking about spiritual matters and, the account continues, he did so with such eloquence that all 'were rapt in God by the overabundance of divine grace that descended upon them'.

While they sat in mystical rapture, citizens in Assisi thought that they saw something like an immense fire burning near St Mary of the Angels. They rushed down to help put it out but, when they arrived, they only saw Francis, Clare and their companions sitting in an ecstatic trance. They concluded that 'it had been a heavenly and not a material fire that God had miraculously shown them to symbolize the divine love which was burning in the souls of those holy friars and nuns'.

Later, 'after a long while', Francis, Clare and their companions 'came back to themselves'. They felt so refreshed by spiritual food, the account concludes, that they had no need to eat the meal set before them.

Beyond the Alps

In these early years, Francis confined his missions to nearby regions such as Umbria and Tuscany. Still, these short forays attracted many men to his order. In the city of Ascoli Piceno, in the Marches of Ancona, for example, he recruited 30 individuals in one visit.

But Francis's word was spreading, especially as he and the brothers travelled outside Italy. Before the close of 1215, Franciscans could be found not only in north and central Italy, but also in southern France and Spain. Furthermore, people were warming up to the 'Little Poor Man', as people were calling him. Upon his arrival in some towns, church bells rang and people greeted him, shouting, *'Ecco il santo!'* ('The saint is here!')

Gifts started pouring in, as well. Giovanni di Velita, lord of Greccio, gave the brothers part of his farm above the Reiti Valley as a hermitage. After hearing Francis preach, Count Roland, lord of Chuisi-in-Casentino, gave Francis a tract of land on top of Mount La Verna to use for prayer and contemplation.

Even nature itself seemed to warm to Francis. Once, when travelling through the Spoleto valley, says Thomas of Celano, Francis saw a large number of birds – doves, crows and magpies – gathered. He rushed up to greet them, as he usually did. But this time, the birds did not fly away, as they always had in the past. So he preached to them: 'My brother birds, you should gently praise your Creator, and love him always.'

Another time, Francis was trying to preach in the village of Alviano, when a flock of swallows started shrieking and chirping. They were so loud that Francis could not be heard. So he turned to the birds and said, 'My sister swallows, now it is time for me also to speak, since you have said enough.

'He used to view the largest crowd of people as if it were a single person, and he would preach fervently to a single person as if to a large crowd.'

THOMAS OF CELANO
ON FRANCIS'S
PREACHING, *THE
LIFE OF ST FRANCIS*,
1228–29

Listen to the word of the Lord, and stay quiet until the word of the Lord is completed.'

'Immediately,' says Thomas of Celano, 'those birds fell silent – to the amazement and surprise of all present – and did not move from that place until the sermon was over.'

Council of the pope

In November 1215, Pope Innocent III opened the Fourth Lateran Council. He addressed 400 bishops and archbishops, 800 abbots and prelates, and ambassadors from all over Europe. After deploring the Muslim Saracens for profaning sacred sites in the Holy Land, Innocent turned his sights on the church. He castigated bishops and priests for their greed, sloth and lust. He recalled Ezekiel's famous vision in which God, his patience exhausted, tells his messenger, 'Go through the city, through Jerusalem, and put a mark [literally, a "Tau"] on the foreheads of those who sigh and groan over the abominations that are committed within it' (Ezekiel 9:4).

His words inspired many a resolution: against the heretical Cathari; for the establishment of more theological schools; commands to the faithful to confess and receive the eucharist at least once a year. And delegates passed a host of rules to check the greed and ambition of prelates.

Innocent was also concerned about the explosion of new orders and spiritual movements. Some were clearly heretical, such as the Cathari, but some were clearly not, such as the Franciscans and Dominicans (another reform order similar to that of Francis). Many of these groups were unknowns, and it

An illuminated initial of a Dominican saint, perhaps Dominic himself.

was difficult to keep track of, much less give adequate guidance to, such enthusiasts. Yet, without oversight, such groups easily fell into heresy. Some abused their followers by insisting they practise severe austerities; others fleeced locals to support their religious work. More fearful of potential dangers than possible good, Innocent announced a moratorium: his office would approve no more new orders. And in the future, aspirants could only enter orders that had steady and secure sources of income.

This put Francis's growing, but still unofficial, order in a bind. Francis still insisted that begging was to be the only source of income for the order. Yet he was also anxious for papal approval. The impasse was temporarily solved by Bishop Guido who, through his connections, made sure that papal authorities still gave unofficial support to Francis.

Priests and bishops largely ignored the council's sweeping resolutions demanding reform. But the climate of reform created by Innocent greatly encouraged the rising mendicant orders such as that of Francis and Dominic. In fact, from this time on, Francis adopted the Tau (the Hebrew letter that is shaped like a uppercase 'T') as his personal emblem, to signal his devotion to Innocent's reforms. He used it as a signature, painted it on his door and placed it in his writings. Some of his followers had visions of Francis with the Tau marked on his forehead.

'[Francis] admonished the brothers not to judge anyone, not to look down upon those who live with refinement and dress extravagantly or fashionably. For, he would say, their God is ours.'

THE LEGEND OF THE THREE COMPANIONS, 1241–47

Missionary outlook

Just as King Arthur gathered his Knights of the Round Table annually at Pentecost, so Francis assembled his brothers at the Portiuncula. In the early years, he held these 'general chapters' twice a year – in spring, at Pentecost, and in September, at the Feast of St Michael. As the order grew and spread geographically, the brothers could gather only once every three years. On these occasions, Francis renewed friendships with companions who had been travelling, updated the Rule, and gave fatherly advice to the brothers.

The general chapters of 1217 and 1219 discussed expansion. The order had continued to grow numerically (it was probably as large as 3,000 by 1219) and spread geographically. As a result, the brothers felt that they needed more structure. They divided themselves into 12 provinces, and a minister provincial was appointed for each. Later, provinces were subdivided into custodies, presided over by *custos*, and below them came residences, hermitages and friaries, under the jurisdiction of 'guardians'. Francis was not enthusiastic about these administrative layers; he knew the temptations that would come with offices of authority. So he insisted that provincials and guardians think of themselves as servants, or as mothers, to those under their care.

At the chapter of 1217, the order decided to make its first concerted effort to reach out beyond Italy. Unfortunately, enthusiasm to spread the gospel outpaced the brother's preparations for foreign missions.

Most of the brothers, usually sent out in pairs, were ignorant of the language and customs of the countries to which they were sent. They went forth, as Francis demanded, without money and without permission to receive it. They had no letters of recommendation from pope, bishop, count or lord. Though the brothers went forth enthusiastically, Bishop Ugolino, a realist, only rebuked Francis: 'Why have you sent your friars to such distant places to die of hunger and undergo other hardships?' Undergo hardships they did.

The missionaries to Hungary thought they had received a stroke of providence when they ran into a Hungarian bishop on their way to his homeland. But once they arrived, he deserted the mission and, left on their own, they were treated cruelly. People thought that they were charlatans who had come to exploit them. Citizens drove them from their cities; farmers set their dogs on them; shepherds poked them with sticks.

The 60 or so friars who made it to Germany fared no better. Not one of them spoke the local language – except for the word '*ja*' ('yes'). They used the word with great success one night when they were hungry. When asked a question, they replied, '*Ja*,' and they received an ample meal. So the next day, wh en they were asked a question, they replied, 'Ja,' but this time people backed away. They later discovered that they had been asked if they were the heretics who had been corrupting Lombardy and were now going to corrupt Germany. The rumour spread that they were the dreaded Cathari, and they found themselves inexplicably arrested, bound naked to the pillory and whipped until they bled. Once freed, they fled the country.

There were exceptions. The friars who preached in Portugal were treated suspiciously at first. But Queen Urraca saw what they were about, and the royal family soon granted them protection. But, overall, these missions were a failure. The brothers returned to Italy miserable and discouraged.

Through trial and error, the brothers slowly learned the keys to foreign missionary work. The next time that Franciscans ventured into Germany (in 1221), for example, they went in small groups so that they would not look like an invading army. They were more patient, attempting only slowly to win people over, to make recruits and to found friaries. In a few years, Franciscans had established themselves not only in Germany, but even farther afield, in Bohemia, Poland, Romania and Norway.

A missionary sermon

The essence of a typical Franciscan evangelistic sermon can be found in the Earlier Rule, in which Francis says that friars should preach following message:

Fear and honour, praise and bless, give thanks and adore the Lord God Almighty in Trinity and Unity, Father, Son, and Holy Spirit, the Creator of all.

Do penance, performing worthy fruits of penance because we shall soon die. Give and it will be given to you. Forgive and you shall be forgiven. If you do not forgive people their sins, the Lord will not forgive you yours. Confess all your sins.

Blessed are those who die in penance, for they shall be in the kingdom of heaven. Woe to those who do not die in penance, for they shall be children of the devil whose works they do, and they shall go into everlasting fire. Beware and abstain from every evil and persevere in good till the end.

England was the scene of another successful mission. In September 1224, nine brothers landed in Dover. Some settled in Canterbury, others in London and others still in Oxford. Many Oxford students and professors immediately joined the order. When they began building a friary together, bystanders were amazed to see a former high prelate carrying stones and mortar like a mason's apprentice. Some Franciscan university students refused to wear shoes even in winter, trudging through snow to classes. Of the three friars who took up residence at the friary, one was so lame that the others had to carry him to prayers. But the group was so overcome with joy at this new life that their prayers were sometimes punctuated with gales of holy laughter.

The first English novice recruited was Brother Solomon. The young man had a reputation for enjoying the finer things of life, but he now happily went begging with bowl in hand, as the Rule required. Once, he knocked on his sister's door. She handed him some bread but turned her face away and exclaimed, 'Cursed be the hour I ever saw you thus!' For Brother Solomon, this was a defining moment. He took the bread with joy and noted that he was being treated by his family as Francis had been treated by his.

The English order gained a reputation for humility and apostolic poverty. They were more commonly known as the Brethren of the Order of the Apostles. Within 10 years of their arrival in England, Franciscans counted some of the country's leading men in their ranks and, 20 years after that, they had 49 friaries in the region.

'As you announce peace with your mouth, make sure that greater peace is in your hearts.'

FRANCIS, TO HIS
BROTHERS BEFORE
SENDING THEM OUT
TO PREACH

Preaching to non-Christians

At the chapter of 1219, Francis raised the stakes and enlisted the order in a more challenging mission still: the evangelization of pagan lands. Since the end of 1212, Francis had tried unsuccessfully to take his message to non-Christian lands. On the way to Syria, winds prevented his ship from completing the voyage. On the way to Morocco two years later, illness thwarted his plans and forced a return home. After 1219, though, Franciscans in general had better success at getting to pagan lands, although they still had no success at winning converts.

Brother Giles, for example, headed for Muslim Tunis. But when the few Christians already there heard about his arrival, they forced him to board a ship and head home. They thought that his zeal would not only get him into trouble with the authorities, but that he would get them into trouble, as well. They were probably right: Giles did not hide his desire – a desire shared by many of the early brothers, including Francis – for martyrdom, the ultimate sacrifice for Christ.

The five brothers who went to Morocco got their wish, but less because of innocent devotion to Christ and more because of their offensive behaviour. When they arrived in Seville, still under the power of the Moors, they entered a mosque and began preaching against the Qur'an. This was as much an offence then as it is today. The worshippers immediately threw them out and beat them. Unfazed, the brothers next went to the royal palace and, when the prince discovered what their mission was, he had them arrested and taken in chains to a tower. From there, the brothers shouted down to passers-by that Mohammed was an imposter and, when they were moved to other quarters, they attempted to convert their jailers and other prisoners.

When they appeared before the local magistrate, he gave them the choice of returning to Italy or being exiled in Morocco. They choose the latter and, shortly after they arrived, they were arrested again. This time, they were whipped and tortured, but they refused to recant, and they foolishly persisted in despising the Qur'an. The local prince, Miramolin, threatened them with death, but they reportedly replied, 'Our bodies are in your power, but our souls are in the power of God!' With that, Miramolin had them beheaded. They were the first Franciscan martyrs, but they do not seem to have represented what was best in the order.

Francis, meanwhile, had appointed two brothers – Matthew of Narni and Gregory of Naples – as vicars to lead the order while he was away. He then headed to the port of

Next page: Louis IX, one of the most famous members of the Franciscan Third Order, was taken prisoner and ransomed during the Seventh Crusade. Fourteenth-century French manuscript illumination by Guillaume de Saint-Pathus.

St Louis as a
prisoner during
the Seventh
Crusade in 1250.
Fourteenth-
century French
manuscript
illumination.

Ancona, with a large group of brothers accompanying him. He intended to catch a ship conveying crusaders to the East. He wanted to make his way to the Muslim sultan in Egypt to preach to him and convert him.

Francis found his ship, but it did not have room for all the brothers. So Francis called to a young boy playing on the wharf and told him to pick 12 friars at random. These, Francis said, were the ones whom God wished to accompany him. They set sail in June 1219. (Francis often resorted to such arbitrary methods to determine the will of God. Once, when he and Brother Masseo came to a fork in the road,

Francis spun Masseo around and around until he dizzily dropped to the ground. The direction in which Masseo ended up, Francis determined, was the direction God wanted them to go. Francis is often praised for such childlike trust in God's providence. But, as the order grew, this method of determining God's direction for the order only threw it into deep confusion.)

Crusades update

The Crusades had been going on for a little more than a century. They began with Pope Urban II's 1095 call for Christians to regain control of Jerusalem from the Saracens. 'A horrible tale has gone forth,' he exhorted his listeners at a church council. 'An accursed race utterly alienated from God… has invaded the lands of the Christians and depopulated them by the sword, plundering, and fire.' He wanted to return Jerusalem to its rightful Lord – Jesus – and, while he was at it, to humiliate the infidels: 'Tear that land from the wicked race and subject it.' The listeners were so taken with the speech that they began shouting, *'Deus vult! Deus vult!'* ('God wills it!'). This, in fact, became the battle cry of the crusaders.

There were eight major crusades in all, between 1096 and 1291, and dozens of minor crusading expeditions. In the First Crusade, the Christians recaptured Jerusalem, but it was only a few decades before this was again lost, and the rest of crusade history was concerned with getting it back.

By the time of the Fifth Crusade, the one which Francis joined, the Saracen Ayyubid dynasty controlled nearly the entire Levantine coast, from Byzantium to Egypt. The only exception were pockets in the Holy Land where Europeans maintained some sovereignty. The sultan at that time, al-Adil, had denied the crusaders access to Palestine, so the crusaders had switched their objective. They planned to attack the Saracen's main port and power base in Egypt, Damietta.

After arriving in Acre, Francis took Illuminato, one of the brothers, with him and sailed next for the crusader camp at Damietta, at the tip of the Nile Delta. They arrived there in late July. The crusaders had been besieging the city (population 80,000) for a year with little success. For several months, Francis and Illuminato remained with the troops, some 40,000 strong (not counting another 20,000 nurses, cooks, pilgrims, sightseers, beggars and other civilians). By their preaching and charm, they won the admiration of many, some of whom, in fact, joined the order then and there.

The two brothers also helped to tend the sick. In the

Questioning admirer

Jacques de Vitry, then bishop of Acre, has left us a first-hand account of Francis's ministry in Egypt. He had first bumped into Franciscan brothers in Rome a few years earlier. He had been thoroughly impressed. 'They are in no way occupied with temporal things,' he wrote, 'but with fervent desire and ardent zeal, they labour each day to draw from the vanities of the world souls that are perishing, and draw them to their way of life.'

De Vitry had arrived in Acre in November 1216 to take up his new bishopric in the Holy Land. By the next autumn, armies of the Fifth Crusade were gathering in Acre to prepare for an assault on Damietta. A year after that, de Vitry found himself in Damietta to assist with the siege. He remained there until the end of the campaign in 1221.

In a letter to friends back in Acre, he noted Francis's effectiveness as an evangelist, but not without a bit of concern. He complained that a prior of one of his churches was leaving his post to join the order, as had two others whom he had put in charge of another church. In addition, his English clerk had abandoned him for the order. De Vitry then added, 'I am having a difficult time holding on to the cantor… and several others.'

About the Franciscans, he wrote, 'By our way of thinking, this order is quite risky, because it sends out two by two throughout the world, not only formed religious, but also immature young men who should first be tested and subjected to conventual discipline for a time.' Though de Vitry was an ardent admirer of Francis, and was disgusted with church corruption, he recognized how Francis's methods made things more difficult for loyal churchmen such as himself.

summer heat, epidemics of disease and dysentery swept through the crusader camp, and septicaemia and gangrene inflicted the wounded. November brought torrential rains and a strong north wind, which drove the sea inland, flooding the camp. Corpses of fish, donkeys, horses, and even of men and women, floated about. In the winter months, an outbreak of scurvy killed 10,000 people. Francis and Illuminato were kept very busy.

At the end of the summer of 1219, Francis finally convinced the papal legate to let him cross enemy lines to go to preach to the sultan. The convincing took some doing because, according to the *Chronicle of Ernoul* (whose author, Ernoul, was a shield-bearer for a feudal lord in the Holy Land), the cardinal 'would never want to give them permission to go to a place where they would only be killed'.

Francis and his companion had replied that the cardinal would not be blamed, because he and Illuminato were not asking to be ordered there. They only wanted permission to go. They begged the cardinal insistently until he finally relented.

So Francis and Illuminato headed for the Saracen camp, probably in September 1219, during a truce between the armies. When Saracen sentinels spotted them, of course, they seized them and dragged them before the sultan. The sultan asked them if they had come with a message from the Christian army. Or perhaps they had come to convert to Islam. (Both Muslims and Christians crossed lines to join the faith of their enemies.)

Francis and Illuminato replied that they had come as messengers of the Lord God. They said that they were hoping that the sultan might convert to Christianity. According to the *Chronicle of Ernoul* they said, 'If you wish to believe us, we will hand over your soul to God, because we are telling you in all truth that if you die in the law which you now profess, you will be lost and God will not possess your soul.' They then laid down a challenge: if the sultan would call in 'the most learned teachers of your realm', Francis and Illuminato would convince them that their religion was false.

Ernoul may be a little confused here. Dominicans would attempt to use reason to argue another out of his religion. But that was never the way with Francis. Most likely, he simply wanted to preach his standard message of penance. In his Rule, in fact, he expressly told his brothers 'not to engage in arguments or disputes' but instead to simply 'announce the Word of God… in order that [unbelievers] may believe in God, the Father, the Son, and the Holy Spirit'.

Whatever it was that Francis wanted to say, he never had a chance to say it. When the sultan assembled his 'highest nobles and wisest men' and explained the reason for the gathering, the Muslim teachers – conservatives, if not fundamentalists – balked.

'Lord, you are the sword of the law,' they reminded the sultan. 'You have the duty to maintain and defend it.' They went on: 'The law forbids giving a hearing to preachers [of another religion],' adding that anyone who spread a faith other than Islam should be killed.

'It is for this reason', they concluded, 'that we command you, in the name of God and the law, that you have their heads cut off immediately, as the law demands.' With that, they stormed out of the room.

After only what could have been an awkward silence, the sultan turned to Francis and Illuminato. He assured them that he was not going to behead them. He tried, in fact, to put the best face on things. 'That would be an evil reward for me to bestow on you,' he said, 'who conscientiously risked death in order to save my soul for God.' He then said that if they decided to remain in his care, he would give them 'vast lands and many possessions'. This may have been an exaggerated offer of Middle Eastern hospitality. It may have been a test of their sincerity.

The two brothers replied bluntly that they no longer wished to stay, since it was clear that the sultan had no intention of converting. They only asked to be allowed return safely to the Christian camp. The sultan then offered them presents of gold, silver and silk garments before they left but, again, they refused. A meal would be a sufficient gift to send them on their way. They were then escorted safely back to the Christian army.

Francis escaped his martyrdom only by luck or God's providence. Like the brothers in Morocco, he did nearly everything wrong. He began preaching his message without earning the right to be heard. He offended the religious leaders. He insulted the hospitality of his host. How he got away cleanly is nothing less than a miracle.

Francis, however, probably thought himself a failure. He failed to convert the sultan – and neither did he suffer martyrdom. Francis was, no doubt, further discouraged by the military turn of affairs. By January 1220, Damietta was on its last legs – a mere 3,000 emaciated men, women and

Francis preaches to the Egyptian sultan and other Muslims. Altar panel attributed to Bonaventura Berlinghieri in the Bardi chapel, Santa Croce, Florence.

children remained alive in the city. When the crusaders entered it, they beat and raped the remaining adults, and then sold them into slavery. They then spent three months arguing about who was going to control which part of the city.

On top of that, Francis's physical health had seriously deteriorated. Nursing, preaching and prayer, combined with the unsanitary conditions in the Nile region, had worn him down. He had contracted an eye disease, probably trachoma, an infection spread by flies, which chronically inflames the underside of the eyelids. This disease would plague him for the rest of his life.

Sometime in early 1220, he returned to Acre, and then wandered about the Holy Land for months. Where he went and what he did, we do not know. It is not unlikely that he went about in deep discouragement, trying to discern what God would have him do next.

One day during these wanderings, he ran into a brother who probably embraced him enthusiastically. Some people in Italy suggested that Francis's long stay away could only mean he had been killed, so the brother was overjoyed to see him. The brother then blurted out some astonishing news: the order had forsaken his ideals and was in complete disarray.

Francis now knew what he needed to do next. He made preparations to return to the Portiuncula immediately.

Francis in Conflict, Order in Conflict

By the general chapter of 1219, it was clear that the innocence and naivety of the early years were over for the Franciscan Order. A simple Rule for a dozen men, living together in humble dwellings, guided by a charismatic leader was one thing, but now there were thousands of people, from many parts of Europe. Some of them had had no contact with the founder. Many had never been nurtured and shaped by his ideals.

So why did they join? Some simply preferred the order's companionship to their families or to a solitary life. Others were taken with the humility and friendliness of the early friars. Others seemed to have simply misunderstood what the order was about. They imagined that, like other orders of the day, the rule would be moderate and that they would have opportunity for study. Some even thought that a stint in the order would bode well for their church careers.

With this mixture of motives and members, it was inevitable that some would begin to chafe at the Rule. Many brothers who had been appointed superiors or ministers had been outstanding or influential clerics before joining the order. They soon resented having to obey an uneducated man such as Francis. And age-old class distinctions were difficult to erase.

Thomas of Celano tells a story of Francis and Brother Leonardo as they returned from an overseas mission. They were both exhausted from their travels. Francis rode on their donkey while Leonardo led it by the reigns. Leonardo, whose family's standing in Assisi had been much higher than that of Francis's family, began to grumble to himself.

'His parents and mine did not socialize as equals, and here he is riding while I am on foot leading this donkey.' Francis, sensing Leonardo's resentment, said, 'Brother, it is not right that I should ride while you go on foot, for in the world you were more noble and influential than I.' Leonardo felt ashamed and begged forgiveness.

Francis's personal charm and humility could disarm such resentment but, as the order grew, he was not able to intervene every time that human nature threatened to disrupt things. At the chapter of 1219, a number of brothers made no effort to conceal their concerns about the order. They wanted the order to be more like the other religious orders of the day. This would allow them to study more, to adhere to a more moderate poverty and to take advantage of the influence of prelates (for example, getting letters of introduction so that they could more easily preach in new regions).

External pressures

In addition to these internal tensions, there was pressure from outside. Since early in 1217, Pope Honorius had appointed Ugolino, bishop of Ostia, as his legate in northern Italy. Ugolino gained recruits for the next crusade, kept an eye on German incursions, enforced the decrees of the Fourth Lateran Council and supervised religious houses in his province.

Ugolino took this last responsibility especially seriously. He was described once as a man 'afire' with love for Francis. Thomas of Celano, in *The Life of St Francis*, wrote of him, 'When he saw that Francis despised all earthly things more than the rest, and that he was alight with the fire that Jesus had sent upon the earth, his soul was from that moment knit with the soul of Francis, and he devoutly asked his prayers and most graciously offered his protection to him in all things.' He sometimes donned the dress of Francis and walked about barefoot with Francis and his brothers. He wanted Francis's order, and that of Clare, who also deeply impressed him, to grow and remain strong.

'Those who do not wish to taste how sweet the Lord is and who love the darkness more than the light, not wishing to fulfil God's commands, are cursed; it is said of them by the prophet, "Cursed are those who stray from your commands."'

FRANCIS, IN AN
ADMONITION TO HIS
BROTHERS UPON
HIS RETURN FROM
SYRIA IN 1220

But he differed with Francis about how to ensure that. In this regard, he was probably more realistic about human nature and church politics than was Francis. It is also fair to say that many of his decisions saved the order for future generations. The only problem was that, at the time, his decisions thwarted some elements of Francis's original vision.

He was not happy with the Rule's contempt of owning property, handling money, gaining papal favours and practising judicious planning. In *this* world, he reasoned, such things were necessary if the order was to survive. He was especially troubled about Clare and her sisters at San Damiano. He was anxious to take steps to maintain their orthodoxy, find regular means to support their house, and protect their virginity in a cruel and capricious society.

Bishop Guido had for some time put pressure on Francis to avoid becoming an excessive burden on others, especially now that the order numbered more than 1,000. No more relying on the generosity of a lazaret, a priest or a citizen to house them; they were to construct their own shelters, he had said.

Francis felt caught. On the one hand, he had more than once preached and acted against such property ownership. The most dramatic example, told in *Mirror of Perfection*, came at one of the annual general chapters, probably the chapter of 1219 or 1221. Francis had been travelling as preparations were being made for the chapter, and the Commune of Assisi, knowing that the order had been growing dramatically, erected a large building of stone and mortar to house many of the brothers while they attended the chapter. When Francis arrived, he was astonished – he thought that the brothers had built a huge house for their own comfort. This was a far cry from the simple thatch huts that had characterized their life.

He immediately climbed up on the roof of the house and ordered some brothers to join him. They began, one by one, to lift the tiles from the roof and toss them to the ground. Francis intended to dismantle the building completely. Some knights of Assisi, who helped with crowd control at these chapters (in these years, many sightseers would gather to watch the brothers), approached Francis. 'Brother, this house belongs to the Commune of Assisi,' they explained. 'And we are here to represent the Commune. We forbid you to destroy our house.' Francis stopped and looked at the knights. 'If the house is yours,' he said, 'I will not touch it.' And immediately he and the other friars descended.

On the other hand, Francis recognized the wisdom of Guido's advice. He did not want to be a burden to others, so he sought a middle ground. The brothers could build huts

The ornate lower church of Basilica San Francesco in Assisi.

for themselves for private prayer, he said, but nothing elaborate. They could construct only 'poor houses of wood and plaster' (bricks, stones and tiles were forbidden). And the property was to be surrounded not by a high wall (typical of the day), but simply by a hedge. For corporate prayer, chapels could be erected, but not big churches.

Francis still did not want the brothers to own holy or service books, such as New Testaments or missals. He felt that owning things would eventually lead to indolence and pride. One story in *The Assisi Compilation* describes an incident when a brother was badgering Francis for a book of Psalms of his own. Francis replied, 'And when you have a Psalter, you will want a breviary, and when you have a breviary, you will install yourself in a chair like a great prelate, and you will order your brother, "Bring me my breviary!"'

On the other hand, he wanted his brothers to pray the offices and read the Psalms. So he compromised. The Dominican-style, large books used for study, were forbidden. But Franciscans could have tiny versions, no bigger than the palm of a hand, and which could easily be tucked in a sleeve.

Francis's departure

It is no accident that Francis chose this time to embark on his longest missionary journey – his trip to Syria after the chapter of 1219. He may have had more than Muslim evangelism on his mind. He may have longed to escape the headaches of administrating an order that required more and more compromises. It is clear, in retrospect, that leaving was a mistake. And his taking with him Peter Cantanii was another. If Peter had stayed behind and acted as one of the order's vicars, he might have prevented the confusion that set in under the leadership of vicars Gregory of Naples and Matthew of Narni (relative newcomers to the order).

It was not long before a wave of insecurity swept over the order. After a few months' absence, it was rumoured that Francis was dead. So Gregory and Matthew took it upon themselves to bring a little more discipline to the order. They multiplied fasts and prescribed many privations that went beyond the spirit of the Rule. To speed up missionary work, the vicars solicited favours from the Roman Curia and letters of commendation.

On top of that, some friars moved into permanent buildings. In Bologna, for example, the provincial Peter

'Francis's decision to leave [Italy in 1219] must have… been instinctive, an act of impulse or faith, which changed both him and his family, for better or worse, irreversibly.'

ADRIAN HOUSE,
*FRANCIS OF ASSISI:
A REVOLUTIONARY
LIFE*, 2000

Staccia became envious of the great educational facilities
owned by the Dominicans. Peter had held a chair in
jurisprudence before joining the order, and he had a high
view of education. Francis had bent his rules to allow Peter
to supervise a number of brothers who wanted to study
the Bible and liturgy. But now Peter went too far; he had
accepted, on behalf of the brothers (and with the approval of
the vicars), a large building where they could live and study.

Bishop Ugolino, for his part, decided that it was time to
enforce some of his ideas. He imposed on Clare's order, and
on all the women's communities in his province, his own
rule – the *Constitutions*. This rule said that each convent
must have a Visitor, or informal inspector, connected with
it. For Clare, who had enjoyed regular visits, but only from
Francis's brothers, this must have been a hard obedience.

All this was too much for friars who had been with
Francis since the early years. Many raised their voices in
protest. Others refused to submit to the vicars' orders.
Others still refused to live in community and just wandered
about longing for their shepherd and guide.

Francis's return

As Francis returned from the Holy Land, he knew that
things were out of control. He also realized that, alone, he
would not be able to rein things in. Before he had left the
Holy Land, he had asked two brothers – Elias, provincial
minister of Syria, and Caesar, a diligent scribe – to join
him. Francis had sized up the two men and recognized
that their strong leadership was needed to help him.

But Francis knew that even this would not be enough.
Sometime earlier he had had a dream, which turned out
to be a premonition of things to come. In the dream, he
saw a small, black hen, with feathered legs but with the
feet of a dove. It had so many chicks that it was unable to
gather them all under its wings, so they wandered about in
circles. Francis came to understand the dream. As he later
explained, 'I am that hen: short in stature, and dark by
nature. I must be simple like a dove, flying up to heaven

with the feathered strokes of virtue. The Lord in his mercy has given, and will give me, many sons whom I will be unable to protect with my own strength.'

As he was returning to the fractured order, he concluded, 'I must, therefore, commend them to the holy church who will protect and guide them under the shadow of her wings.'

So, before he returned to Assisi, Francis headed for Rome. He found Bishop Ugolino, and together they went before the pope. Francis knew that Ugolino had enforced some decisions that were not in the spirit of the order. But he believed that Ugolino had the best interests of the order at heart. Francis saw that now that his order numbered in the thousands, Rome would be increasingly tempted to dictate policy, and that Francis's ideals of radical poverty

Elias: black sheep of the order

Elias was a man of remarkable gifts, possessing a character that was an ironic combination of faith and pride. He was a notary in the town of Bologna when he joined Francis, and he quickly became a trusted friend. Francis placed great confidence in him, perhaps because of Elias's organizing genius. Elias was appointed provincial of the friars in Syria and, in 1221, minister general of the entire order.

Elias was close to Francis in his last years. According to Thomas of Celano in *The Life of St Francis*, he received Francis's dying blessing: 'You are my son. I bless above all and throughout all.' At Francis's death, the grieving Elias gathered witnesses to verify Francis's stigmata and wrote the letter informing friars of their founder's passing.

But he seems to have misunderstood his mentor's message of poverty. After Francis's death, he completed the ornate lower church of the great basilica that today dominates Assisi. As minister general, he became an autocrat, appointing, transferring and dismissing provincials without hesitation. On the grounds of personal health, he insisted on having a personal cook, and he wanted his servants to wait upon him in proper attire.

Conservatives finally orchestrated a coup in 1239, and Elias was deposed. He joined the perpetual papal enemy, Frederick II, and was then excommunicated. But a small body of friars stuck with him and, for them, he erected a monastery at Cortona.

Ugolino: machiavellian reformer

It is not surprising that Francis, when he was looking for a papal representative to help bring order to the Franciscans, asked for Bishop Ugolino. Though Francis's biographers refer continually to Ugolino's humility, history mostly remembers him as a wily political animal. This did not become evident until he became Pope Gregory IX in 1227. At the time, the West was in the middle of a crusade to the East. But Emperor Frederick II was having second thoughts, and had decided not to lead an offensive. When the freshly installed Gregory heard this, he excommunicated Frederick. The tactic worked, and Frederick relented and left for Palestine. Gregory then lifted the excommunication – but went on to have his papal armies attack Frederick's Italian lands. When Frederick hurried back to recover his territory, Gregory excommunicated him again for deserting the crusade!

Ugolino is also the pope with the dubious distinction of founding the Inquisition. He did so, giving special responsibility to the Dominicans, in order to combat heresy. But Gregory was a complex man and, all the while, he was fostering the growth of the Franciscans, the Poor Clares and the Dominicans. Indeed, helping these orders only enhanced his power as pope, since they were directly accountable to him. Yet he also knew that they could reform the church from the bottom up, just as he was trying to reform the church from the top down.

Pope Gregory IX Consecrating the Chapel of Subiaco (14th-century fresco) by Consolo.

and simplicity would be undermined. Rather than trust his order to the capricious nature of papal politics, he asked the pope to make Ugolino protector of his order. To this, the pope agreed.

Francis and Ugolino immediately sat down to talk. Francis explained why he objected to a number of Ugolino's decisions. Ugolino relented on a few matters, and Francis also compromised. The two friars, Gregory and Matthew, would be posted elsewhere. Their amendments to the Rule would be struck. Brothers who had branched out on their own (such as John of Capella, who had organized a sub-order composed solely of lepers) would be censured. And papal letters of introduction would be given to all missionary brothers, to ease their way into new territories.

Francis's resignation

In addition to these agreements, Francis said that he was going to step down as head of the order. He saw that he was not the man to lead the order through its next stage. He would turn matters over to Peter Cantanii.

When he announced this at the next general chapter, in September 1220, many brothers wept openly. But Francis refused to change his mind, and he symbolically bowed before Peter to indicate his new authority. He also asked Peter to appoint him a companion, 'who will represent your authority to me and whom I shall obey as if I were obeying you'. He did this, he said, as a 'good example and for love of the virtue of obedience'.

The early biographers make Francis's relinquishing of leadership look easy. It must have been anything but that. His early ambitions for a large brotherhood that would redeem the world were being fulfilled. But he found himself incapable of negotiating the new situation, which demanded organization, financial accountability and the wise use of church politics. Such things, Francis knew all too well, were not his forte. Even worse – they were the very things he had stood against when he started his order a little over a decade earlier. He was simply mystified as to how he personally could retain his ideals while providing for a growing order. He decided that he could not, and he turned matters over to others whom he trusted.

But he would never, for the rest of his life, be able to keep his hands out of things. Though Francis promised to obey other minister generals who presided over the order, he always made his presence and ideals known. For example, he was forever telling his friars to distrust learning: 'A great cleric must in some way give up his

learning when he comes to the order, that he may offer himself naked to the arms of the cross.' Another time, he said, 'My brothers who are being led by their curious passion for learning will find their hands empty on the day of retribution when books, no longer useful, will be thrown out of windows and into cubby holes.'

He worried that if the brothers spent too much time studying, they would neglect the higher work of prayer and service. Even if in the service of better

St Antony of Padua, the most celebrated early Franciscan preacher, by Alvise Vivarni.

preaching, there could be problems: 'When they have preached to a few men or to the people, and learn that certain ones were edified or converted to penance through their discourse, they are puffed up and pride themselves on the results.'

Still, Ugolino and Elias, minister general after Peter Cantanii died, pushed for more learning. They realized that for all its spiritual temptations, learning was necessary for the long-term success of the order. Though an unschooled Francis could preach with wisdom beyond his education,

St Anthony: Hammer of the Heretics

Today, Anthony of Padua – the popular St Anthony – is widely invoked by Catholics for the return of lost property, for protection during travel and for health during pregnancy. In paintings, we see him with a Bible or a lily in his hand, representing his knowledge of scripture, or with a donkey, which supposedly knelt before the sacrament he once held aloft.

But history shows a more rugged side to Anthony. Born in 1195 in Lisbon to a noble family, he joined and began studying with members of the Augustinian Order at the age of 15. Ten years later, his life was revolutionized.

One day, some relics passed through town. They were the remains of the Franciscan friars who had recently been martyred in Morocco. Anthony was deeply moved and, like many spiritual athletes of the day, nothing excited him more than the thought of dying for Christ. He begged his order to release him from his vows so that he could join the Franciscans. He then convinced the Franciscans to make him a missionary to Morocco.

But on the way to Morocco, a storm forced his ship to Sicily and, from there, he made his way to Assisi. For some reason, he determined that this was where God wanted him to spend the rest of his days in quiet prayer and study.

When he preached at his own ordination, however, listeners were amazed at his eloquence and passion. He was soon given various administrative posts in the order – including being a teacher at Bologna. He also preached, sometimes attracting crowds of up to 30,000 people. His favourite themes were denouncing the elite for their unjust treatment of the poor and the heresies of the Cathari. He became known, in fact, as the 'Hammer of the Heretics'.

From 1230 onwards, he spent the remainder of his life at Padua, and he died at the premature age of 36. He was canonized within six months, an extraordinarily brief time. He was named a Doctor of the Church in 1946.

*'Francis
depended far
too much upon
direct personal
influence
and upon the
hour-to-hour
guidance of the
Holy Spirit. He
could not plan
ahead because
he was never
certain where
God would
lead him.'*

JOHN R. MOORMAN,
*ST FRANCIS OF
ASSISI*, 1950

most friars needed some training if they were to convince hearers of their message.

Francis eventually saw the wisdom of this, at least to some degree. When one particularly gifted brother, Anthony of Padua, was appointed by Elias as a teacher at Bologna, Francis confirmed the decision. He wrote a little note to Anthony: 'I am pleased that you teach sacred theology to the brothers,' adding, 'providing that, as is contained in the Rule, you "do not extinguish the Spirit of prayer and devotion" during study of this kind.'

A new Rule

In 1222, Ugolino and Elias decided that, given the order's new situation, it was time to modify and formalize the Rule. Naturally, they asked Francis to begin to draw up the document. Francis asked brother Bonizzo of Bologna and his companion brother Leo, among others, to help him.

Some of the brothers panicked when they heard this. 'We are afraid that he will make it so difficult that we will not be able to observe it,' they blurted out to Elias. They told Elias to tell Francis they would refuse to obey such a rule: 'He may write it for himself, but not for us!'

Elias went with an escort of brothers to meet with Francis and his companions, who were living at a mountain retreat. When Elias explained what concerned the brothers, Francis lifted his eyes upward and said, 'Lord, did I not tell you that they would not have confidence in you?'

Then, according to *The Assisi Compilation*, a voice from above said, 'Francis, nothing in the Rule comes from you; everything comes from me. I wish this Rule to be observed to the letter, to the letter, to the letter, without gloss, without gloss, without gloss!'

Francis turned to the brothers and said, 'Did you hear? Do you want me to have it repeated?' The brothers, says the chronicler, 'withdrew totally ashamed and striking their breasts'.

The story seems to be a fabrication created by later followers, who were lobbying the order to retain a strict interpretation of the Rule. But it speaks poignantly of the changing nature of the brotherhood, and of the divisions within it. Even Francis could not stop these developments.

The new rule, now called the Later Rule, thus does not have the stamp of Francis's personality and vision, as did the Earlier Rule. It is a document that has gone through the layers of church bureaucracy. It is clear and practical, and is easily memorized, but the poetry and passion of Francis is gone. To be sure, much of the original vision remains. But it also shows evidence of compromise. The command to 'carry nothing for your journey' is absent. The command to return no violence to an offender has been omitted. And the brothers' right to admonish superiors for abuses of office is nowhere to be found.

The compromised version was presented at the next general chapter, in September 1223, and the brothers approved it. In November, Honorius III approved it as the official Rule of the order.

C H A P T E R   1 0

Imitation of Christ

At one point in *The Life of St Francis*, Thomas of Celano sums up the meaning of Francis's life. 'His highest aim, foremost desire and greatest intention', he wrote, 'was to pay heed to the holy gospel in all things and through all things, to follow the teaching of our Lord Jesus Christ and to retrace his footsteps completely with all vigilance and all zeal, all the desire of his soul and all the fervour of his heart.'

Francis insisted that he and his brothers *obey* the commands of their Lord as literally as possible. The habit began early. He read a passage from the Gospels – about Jesus' command that his disciples have only one tunic and no sandals – and Francis took it as a personal command to himself and, later, to his brothers. For Francis, *poverty* was a synonym for *obedience*. Furthermore, poverty meant not only physical poverty, but also a life of self-denial, humility and service to Christ.

Yet obedience was only part of Francis's method. Obedience alone, he recognized, would only lead to legalism and self-righteousness. The Christ-like life demanded something more.

Ardent love was one thing. Francis concluded his Earlier Rule with an extended doxology to his love for God. 'With our whole heart, our whole soul, our whole mind, and with our whole strength and fortitude, with our whole understanding, with all our powers, with every effort, every affection, every feeling, every desire and wish, let us love the Lord God.'

In fact, when he became caught up in this theme, he could hardly control himself:

Wherever we are, in every place, in every hour, at every time of the day, every day and continually, let us truly and

'Inwardly cleansed, interiorly enlightened, and inflamed by the fire of the Holy Spirit, may we be able to follow in the footprints of your beloved Son, our Lord Jesus Christ.'

FRANCIS, A PRAYER
IN *LETTER TO THE
ENTIRE ORDER*,
1225–26

humbly believe, hold in our heart and love, honour, adore, serve, praise, bless, glorify and exalt, magnify and give thanks to the Most High and Supreme Eternal God, Trinity and Unity, Father, Son and Holy Spirit, Creator of all, Saviour of all who believe and hope in him, and love him.

This love for God was focused like a laser beam on the second member of the Trinity. It was Jesus who spoke to Francis from the San Damiano cross. Jesus' words shook Francis out of his materialistic stupor and drove him to take up the life of poverty. And so for Francis, nothing less than imitation of Christ – perfect God and perfect man – would do. The imitation of Christ was the highest aspiration of humankind.

An early passage in the Earlier Rule shows how important this was to Francis right from the beginning of his order: 'The rule and life of these brothers is this, namely: to live in obedience, chastity, and without anything of their own, and to follow in the teaching *and the footsteps* of our Lord Jesus Christ' [emphasis added].

Francis joined obedience to Christ with his love of Jesus; he expressed both by giving himself to a life of pure imitation of Christ. Thus Thomas of Celano notes, 'Francis used to recall with regular meditation the words of Christ and recollect his deeds with most attentive perception.' And as if the reader had not yet understood the point, Thomas adds, 'Indeed, so thoroughly did the humility of the Incarnation and the charity of the Passion occupy his memory that he scarcely wanted to think of anything else.'

The living nativity
When Francis turned over the administration of the order to others in 1220, he spent more time in prayer than ever. And he sought more than ever a perfect imitation of Christ. Two of the most memorable and remarkable incidents of his life occurred during these, his last, years. Each one, in its own way, is a culmination of his desire to imitate Christ in all things.

The first concerned the beginning of Jesus' life on earth. For Francis, few feasts of the church year compared to Christmas. The image of Jesus in his mother's arms made him stammer with emotion. Sometimes he wept when he pondered the poverty into which the Son of God was born. One day, when at a meal, a friar was talking about the humble circumstances of the birth of Jesus,

The good Catholic

Francis was not only enamoured with Christ, but with anything that 'carried' Christ to the rest of humankind – hence his devotion to Mary, Jesus' mother. Thomas of Celano sums it up like this: 'He embraced the Mother of Jesus with inexpressible love, since she made the Lord of Majesty a brother to us. He honoured her with his own praises, poured out prayers to her, and offered her his love in a way that no human tongue can express.'

One song of praise composed by Francis reads, 'Hail, O Lady, Holy Queen, Mary, Holy Mother of God… Hail his palace! Hail his tabernacle! Hail his dwelling!'

Likewise, Francis venerated the church and its priests because, as he believed, they carried Christ in the holy eucharist. Just before he died, Francis dictated a document which is now called *The Testament*, his last admonitions to his brothers. Towards the beginning, he explained once more his relationship to the church:

The Lord gave me, and gives me still such faith in priests who live according to the rite of the holy Roman Church because of their orders that, were they to persecute me, I would still want to have recourse to them… I act in this way because, in this world, I see nothing corporally of the most high Son of God except his most holy body and blood, which they receive and administer to others.

In an undated admonition to his brothers, he nearly equated the Incarnation with the sacrament of Communion: 'As he [Jesus] revealed himself to the holy apostles in true flesh, so he reveals himself to us now in sacred bread… And in this way the Lord is always with his faithful.'

Francis began shaking with sobs. He got up from the table and finished his meal on the dirt floor, in honour of the poverty of Christ's birth.

One time when Christmas fell on a Friday, Brother Morico asked him if they should be eating meat, since Friday was normally a fast day. An indignant Francis replied, 'You sin, brother, when you call Friday the day

'He [Francis] used to observe the nativity of the child Jesus with an immense eagerness above all other solemnities, affirming it was the feast of feasts, when God was made a little child and hung on human breasts.'

THOMAS OF CELANO, *THE LIFE OF ST FRANCIS*, 1228–29

Madonna and Child with Angels by Duccio di Buoninsegna.

when "unto us a child is born". I want even the walls to eat meat on that day, and if they cannot, at least on the outside they be rubbed with grease!'

With such feeling he approached Christmas in 1223. Two weeks prior to the holy feast, he had arranged with his friend, and now disciple, John Velita, lord of Greccio, to allow him the use of a steep hill opposite the town. The slope was dotted with caves and small woods. There, Francis said, he wanted to 'enact the memory of that babe who was born in Bethlehem, to see as much as is possible with my own bodily eyes the discomfort of his infant needs, how he lay in a manger, and how, with an ox and an ass standing by, he rested on hay'. Francis publicized what he was about to do, so that on Christmas Eve both friars and people of the area joined him on his retreat.

Thomas of Celano describes the scene. People carried candles and torches as they wound their way up the mountain. They finally reached the spot where Francis had arranged for a living nativity to be placed, with an ox and a donkey, and hay in the manger, and a baby asleep within. A priest led the group in the Mass, at which Francis assisted in singing the liturgy. He also preached on 'the birth of the poor King and the poor city of Bethlehem'.

'At length,' Thomas concludes, 'the night's solemnities drew to a close and everyone went home with joy,' as 'simplicity is given place of honour, poverty is exalted and humility is commended'.

In this account, Thomas mostly uses the present tense. This suggests that the living nativity had become an annual event at Greccio. Indeed, the custom soon spread throughout Europe. Scholars argue as to whether this was the first living nativity but, at a minimum, it was a custom popularized by Francis – in imitation of Christ.

Stigmata

The second event, shrouded in some mystery, was Francis's imitation of the end of Christ's life. In September 1224,

Francis went with some companions (including Leo and Angelo) on a 40-day retreat on Mount La Verna, the lonely mountain in Tuscany that had been given for his use by Count Orlando 11 years earlier. Sometime about the Feast of the Exaltation of the Cross (on 14 September), Francis, deep in prayer, experienced a vision. He saw an angel with six wings above him, with its arms outstretched and fastened to a cross.

Bonaventure, in *The Major Legend of St Francis*, says that Francis 'rejoiced at the gracious way Christ looked upon him under the appearance of the Seraph, but the fact that he was fastened to a cross pierced his soul with a sword of compassionate sorrow'. Francis meditated on this vision. He eventually understood that he, Francis, was 'to be totally transformed into the likeness of Christ crucified'. It was not to be by the martyrdom he had longed for his whole life, 'but by the enkindling of his soul'.

When the vision departed, says Bonaventure, 'It left in his heart a marvellous fire and imprinted in his flesh a likeness of signs no less marvellous.' Immediately, wounds appeared on his body – one on each hand and each foot, and one on his side – all of which would bleed periodically for the rest of his life.

The marks came to be called *stigmata*, from the Greek word *stigma*, meaning 'brand mark' or 'scar'. The word is found in Paul's letter to the church at Galatia, where he says, 'I carry the marks (*stigmata*) of Jesus branded on my body' (Galatians 6:17). The same word was carried over into the Latin Vulgate translation, the common Bible version of Francis's day. Clearly, in the mind of Francis and his followers, the marks were the final evidence of Francis's imitation of Christ.

At first, Francis tried to hide the marks, even from his closest followers, but they could not but help notice his bleeding as they nursed him when he fell ill. When they pestered him for information about them, he eventually relented and told them what had happened.

'In all things he wished without hesitation to be conformed to Christ crucified, who hung on the cross poor, suffering, and naked.'

BONAVENTURE, *THE MAJOR LEGEND OF ST FRANCIS*, 1260–63

Francis receives
the stigmata –
the culmination
of his desire to
imitate Christ.
*St Francis
Receiving the
Stigmata* by
Giotto di
Bondone.

Other stigmata

Francis was the first person in history to receive the stigmata – but he was not the last. Subsequent Christian history records many people who received the same marks. The most famous in the late Middle Ages were Catherine of Siena (1347–80) and Catherine of Genoa (1447–1510). In the 19th century, some 20 cases were known, including that of Marie de Moerl of Tyrol (1812–68). At the age of 20, she began experiencing spiritual ecstasies which reoccurred regularly for the rest of her life. Louise Lateau of Belgium (1850–83) began nursing victims of cholera at the age of 16, and experiencing ecstasies and the stigmata at the age of 18.

In the 20th century, the most famous stigmatic was Padre Pio. He became a novice of the Capuchin Friars, a Franciscan order, at the age of 15, and became a priest in 1910. At the age of 31, in September 1918, the stigmata appeared on his body as he prayed before a crucifix. The marks remained on him for nearly the rest of his life. Thousands sought him out in Italy to make their confession and to seek his counsel. By the time of his death in 1968, though, the wounds were no longer visible. His beatification is still under consideration by the Vatican.

Over the centuries, some cases of stigmata have proven to be frauds and, in general, the Roman Catholic Church is very slow to recognize or highlight the miraculous nature of the phenomenon.

Nonetheless, he insisted that they keep it as secret as possible. 'Although he tried to hide the treasure found in the field,' remarks Bonaventure, 'he could not prevent some from seeing the stigmata in his hands and feet, although he always kept his hands covered and from that time on always wore shoes.'

By the time of his death, however, some 50 brothers, along with Clare and a number of lay followers, had seen and touched the wounds.

There is no reason to doubt whether Francis had such wounds – the evidence is overwhelming that he did. Besides numerous witnesses, the wounds were described in vivid detail by Thomas of Celano, among others ('marks on the inside of the hands were round, but oblong from the outside, and small pieces of flesh were visible like the points of nails, bent and flattened').

How the wounds came to be is another matter. Some scholars, even Catholics such as the late Herbert Thurston SJ, believe that they can be explained as a physical reaction to intense ecstatic and psychological experiences. Francis so desired to become fully like Christ that his mind convinced his body to produce the wounds of the crucifixion. Others, such as Sr Joanne Schatzlein, a nurse, and Dr Daniel Sulmasy, a physician, conjecture that the wounds may have manifested themselves as a result of Francis's having contracted leprosy and/or tuberculosis. Or perhaps Francis inflicted himself with the wounds, not as an effort to deceive, but as another of his dramatic demonstrations to become a living metaphor of the imitation of Christ.

In the end, it is beyond the ability of science or history to determine the ultimate cause of the stigmata. Francis and his followers certainly believed that the marks were a miracle. More importantly, for Bonaventure, among others, the stigmata completed a spiritual life that had begun with a revelation from a crucifix, and had been devoted to imitating Christ. As Bonaventure put it, 'For the cross of Christ, both offered and taken on by you at the beginning of your conversion and carried continuously from that moment throughout the course of your most proven life... shows with such clarity of certitude that you have finally reached the summit of gospel perfection.'

C H A P T E R   1 1

Brother Sun

In the months following receiving the stigmata, Francis continued to travel, often by donkey because he no longer had the strength to walk, as was his custom. He visited Borgo, San Spolcro, Monte Casale and Citta' di Castello on his way back to the Portiuncula. Then he set out on a preaching tour of Umbria and the Marches. All the while his body deteriorated, especially his stomach, liver and spleen. His eye problems became worse. In spring 1225, he stayed with Clare and her sisters at San Damiano to receive their care.

After much badgering by Brother Elias, now head of the order, Francis agreed to undergo medical treatment. For the rest of his days, Francis would have to endure all sorts of treatments for his eyes. The most brutal consisted of cauterizing with a red-hot iron the flesh around the

Francis is said to have quieted birds when he spoke to them. *St Francis Preaches to the Birds* (c. 1260) by Maestro di San Francesco, fresco in the lower church, Basilica San Francesco, Assisi.

eyes, from ear to eyebrow. But no matter the method, Francis's eyes did not improve. He could not bear sunlight, and even firelight hurt his eyes. He eyes caused him so much pain sometimes that he could not sleep.

As he was wont to do, just when nature was failing him – his body falling apart, his eyes incapable of taking in the beauty of nature – Francis crafted one of the most exquisite poems ever. It was a fitting culmination of one theme that characterized his life and ministry.

Love of nature

We have already noted two incidents in which Francis's presence calmed flocks of birds. These are but two stories that were told about him, starting in his lifetime. Some are quite fantastic, others borrow themes from Greek mythology. The historical authenticity of any one of the Francis nature stories can be debated, but they cannot all be dismissed as fairy tales. The overall picture that emerges from the earliest sources is that Francis had an extraordinary relationship with the created order.

Once, while staying near Greccio, reports Thomas of Celano, a brother brought to Francis a live rabbit caught in a trap. When Francis saw the rabbit, he was 'moved with tenderness'. He said, 'Brother rabbit, come to me. Why did you let yourself get caught?' The brother who had been holding the rabbit let it go, and the rabbit bounded over to Francis and jumped into his arms. Francis, 'caressing it with motherly affection', finally put it down to let it hop back into the woods. After a few hesitant hops, the rabbit turned and bounded back to Francis. This happened again and again until Francis ordered a brother to take the rabbit some distance away before releasing it. Thomas then noted that this also happened with another rabbit when Francis once visited the island on the Lake of Perugia (also known as Lake Trasimeno).

Thomas reports a similar instance with a fish. Once, while he was sitting in a boat on the Lake of Reiti, a fisherman caught a tench (a type of carp) and offered it to

'My brother birds, you should greatly praise your Creator, and love Him always. He gave you feathers to wear, wings to fly, and whatever you need.'

FRANCIS'S SERMON TO THE BIRDS, IN THOMAS OF CELANO, *THE LIFE OF ST FRANCIS*, 1228–29

'From a reflection on the primary source of all things, filled with even more abundant piety, he would call all creatures, no matter how small, by the name of "brother" or "sister".'

BONAVENTURE, *THE MAJOR LEGEND OF ST FRANCIS*, 1260–63

The wolf of Gubbio

The most famous nature story about Francis seems clearly to be a fabrication, but nonetheless it is an example of the type of nature stories that grew up around Francis soon after his death.

A 'fearfully large and fierce wolf', says *The Little Flowers of St Francis*, had been plaguing the town of Gubbio. It was 'rabid with hunger', devouring both animals and man. The townspeople often went into the forest with weapons, 'as if they were going to war', but 'they were not able to escape the sharp teeth and raging hunger of the wolf when they were so unfortunate as to meet'.

When Francis visited the town, he had compassion on the people when they told him their story. He went out to meet the wolf with just one brother as a companion. Upon seeing Francis and his companion, the wolf charged with mouth agape, but Francis made the sign of the cross, and the wolf stopped dead in its tracks.

'Come to me, Brother Wolf,' said Francis, and the wolf obeyed. 'In the name of Christ,' he continued, 'I order you not to hurt me or anyone.' He then lectured the wolf for 'destroying God's creatures without any mercy'. He concluded, 'I want you to promise me that you will never hurt any animal or man.'

The wolf signalled his promise by nodding his head. Francis then took the wolf into town, preached a sermon to both people and wolf, and asked both parties not to hunt one another again. The people voiced their assent, and the wolf gave a visible pledge by raising his right paw. 'From that day,' the story concludes, 'the wolf and the people kept the pact which St Francis made.'

The story is a near-exact match of the Greek myth of Hercules' slaying of the lion. But Hercules' power could resolve the conflict between man and nature only by killing the lion. Francis managed to reconcile man and nature, by the power of Christ.

Francis as a gift. Francis accepted it gladly, calling it 'brother' as he took it in his arms. Then he put it back in the water, blessing God as he did. 'For some time that fish did not leave the spot but stayed next to the boat,' wrote Thomas of Celano, 'playing in the water.' Only when Francis gave it permission to leave did it do so.

Francis seemed to have had a special fondness for sheep. Once, while travelling through the Marches of Ancona with a brother, he came across a man headed for market, carrying two little lambs on his shoulders. Thomas of Celano says that when Francis heard the bleating lambs, he was moved and 'he touched them as a mother does a crying child'.

'Why are you torturing my brother lambs,' Francis asked the man, 'binding and hanging them in this way?'

'I am carrying them to market to sell them, since I need the money,' the man replied.

'What will happen to them?' Francis continued.

The man responded, 'Those who buy them will kill them and eat them.'

'No!' Francis blurted out. 'This must not happen!' He ripped off the cloak, heavy and finely made, that he had borrowed because of the inclement weather. He shoved it towards the man. 'Here, take my cloak as payment and give me the lambs.'

The man, who thought he was getting the better out of the bargain, happily made the trade.

Francis now wondered what in the world he was going to do with the lambs! After getting advice from his companion, he gave the lambs back to the man, but not before making him promise that he would never sell or butcher them.

Even worms became an object of Francis's compassion. One day, he read a text about Jesus that quoted him as saying, 'I am a worm and not a man.' From then on, whenever he saw a worm on the road, he stooped over, picked it up and placed it safely to the side so that it would not be crushed by travellers.

This last story reveals the essence of Francis's ecological

Opposite page: Francis reconciles a vicious wolf and the town of Gubbio. *The Legend of the Wolf of Gubbio* (1437–44) by Sassetto.

Opposite page:
A page from the
medieval
Winchester Bible,
from the middle
of the 12th
century.

sensitivity. It was not an abstract love of nature, or Henry Thoreau's notion (in his essay 'Walking') that 'in wildness is the preservation of the world', that prompted his love of nature. For Francis, nature was a living metaphor for his relationship with God.

He took his cues from the Bible. In the medieval Bible (and Bibles with the Apocrypha today), there was a passage in the book of Daniel that Francis often read: 'The Song of the Three Young Men'. It is a prayer that extols the wonders of the created order – rain, dew, wind, fire, heat, frost, lightning, mountains, plants, birds and so on. Because 'the three young men… invited all the elements to praise and glorify the Creator of all things', says Thomas of Celano, so Francis 'never stopped glorifying, praising and blessing the Creator and Ruler of all things in all elements and creatures'.

Francis delighted in the beauty of flowers because they sprang up from 'the root of Jesse', from the biblical passage that alludes to Christ. By a flower's fragrance, he would say, 'it raised up countless thousands from death'. So, whenever he came across a field of flowers, Thomas of Celano says, he would 'preach to them and invite them to praise the Lord'. He told one friar to save room in his garden for flowers, 'out of love of him who is called the Rose on the plain and the Lily on the mountain slopes'.

Sheep were dear to Francis because they reminded him of Jesus, the Lamb of God, by whose suffering and death salvation was brought into the world. He once spotted a sheep amid a flock of goats, and it immediately brought to Francis's mind an image of Jesus walking meekly and humbly among the Pharisees and chief priests. While Francis was staying at the monastery of San Verecondo, he was told that one of the monastery's newborn lambs had been killed by a sow. 'Alas, brother lamb,' he said, 'innocent animal, always displaying Christ to people!'

'The Canticle of Brother Sun'

It is not surprising, then, that, as his natural body wasted away, Francis turned to the created order to give him

An excerpt from the Song of the Three Young Men

Bless the Lord, all the Lord's creation:
praise and glorify him for ever!...

Bless the Lord, sun and moon,
praise and glorify him for ever!
Bless the Lord, stars of heaven,
praise and glorify him for ever!
Bless the Lord, all rain and dew,
praise and glorify him for ever!
Bless the Lord, every wind,
praise and glorify him for ever!
Bless the Lord, fire and heat,
praise and glorify him for ever!
Bless the Lord, cold and warmth,
praise and glorify him for ever!
Bless the Lord, dew and snowstorm,
praise and glorify him for ever!...

Bless the Lord, mountains and hills,
praise and glorify him for ever!
Bless the Lord, every plant that grows,
praise and glorify him for ever!
Bless the Lord, springs of water,
praise and glorify him for ever!
Bless the Lord, seas and rivers,
praise and glorify him for ever!
Bless the Lord, whales, and everything
that moves in the waters,
praise and glorify him for ever!
Bless the Lord, every kind of bird,
praise and glorify him for ever!
Bless the Lord, all animals wild and
tame,
praise and glorify him for ever!

DANIEL 3:57, 62–68, 75–81

'Everyone says the great problem in Western society today is our collapse of values. For Francis, the supreme value, the value that gave value to everything else, was God.'

CONRAD
HAWKINS OFM,
ST BONAVENTURE
UNIVERSITY,
NEW YORK,
CHRISTIAN HISTORY
MAGAZINE, 1994

perspective. One day, when he had been praying for strength to bear his illnesses, he felt that God spoke to him. 'Be glad and joyful in the midst of your infirmities and tribulations,' the voice said. 'As of now, live in peace, as if you already share in my kingdom.'

The next morning, he told a brother he was determined to 'be full of joy in my infirmities and tribulations'. He was going to 'seek my consolation in the Lord, to give thanks to God the Father, to his only Son our Lord Jesus Christ, and to the Holy Spirit'. He decided there was no better way to do that than to compose a song praising God for his creation. He said, 'Every day we fail to appreciate so great a blessing by not praising as we should the Creator and dispenser of all these gifts.'

The final version of the song, which today is called 'The Canticle of the Creatures' or 'The Canticle of Brother Sun', reads like this:

Most High, all-powerful, good Lord,
  yours are the praises, the glory, the honour, and all blessing.
To you alone, Most High, do they belong,
  and no man is worthy to mention your name.

Praised be you, my Lord, with all your creatures,
  especially Sir Brother Sun,
who is the day and through whom
  you give us light. And he is beautiful and radiant with
    great splendour;
  and bears a likeness of you, Most High One.

Praised be you, my Lord, through Sister Moon and the stars;
  in heaven you formed them clear and precious and
    beautiful.

Praised be you, my Lord, through Brother Wind,
  and through the air, cloudy and serene, and every kind
    of weather,
  through which you give sustenance to your creatures.

Praised be you, my Lord, through Sister Water,
which is very useful and humble and precious
and chaste.

Praised be you, my Lord, through Brother Fire,
through whom you light the night,
and he is beautiful and playful and robust and strong.

Praised be you, my Lord, through our Sister Mother Earth,
who sustains and governs us,
and who produces varied fruits with coloured flowers
and herbs.

Praised be you, my Lord, through those who give pardon for
your love,
and bear infirmity and tribulation.
Blessed are those who endure in peace,
for by you, Most High, they shall be crowned.

A musical product of his age

Despite a lack of radios, CDs and MTV, people in the Middle Ages had plenty of access to music. It was heard and played in both church and street. In the great cathedrals, monks and priests chanted hymns in plainsong, or plainchant – singing with a single melodic line. Since few churches had organs, most singing was done *a cappella*.

Outside of church, kings and noblemen could hire musicians to play harps and lutes for their banquets. Ordinary people sang folk songs, and danced to flutes and drums on their feast days. By 1400, most towns had a civic band of professional musicians, which accompanied official processions and festivals.

Troubadours, travelling musicians and singers, were found all over France and Italy in Francis's day. The songs were often accompanied by a fiddle, which was larger than a modern violin and rested on the musician's lap. The songs were mostly about the glories of romantic love.

Francis loved music from his youth, though we have no indication that he ever learned an instrument. Using the troubadours as his model, as he travelled and preached, he often sang of love, in his case, the love of God. The culmination of a lifetime of his singing in this tradition was his 'Canticle of Brother Sun'.

Praised be you, my Lord, through our Sister Bodily Death,
    from whom no living man can escape.
Woe to those who die in mortal sin.
    Blessed are those whom death will find in your most
        holy will,
            for the second death shall do them no harm.

Praise and bless my Lord and give Him thanks
    and serve Him with great humility.

Francis used this song not just as a personal comfort, but as a means to further the order's mission. He asked Elias to send Brother Pacifico, who had once been the emperor's King of Verse, to take a band of friars around the country to sing it after they preached. They were to end by saying to their audiences, 'We are the Lord's minstrels, and you can repay us for our performance by leading a life of penance.'

When Francis heard that Assisi's podesta and bishop were angrily feuding, he ordered a friar to sing 'The Canticle of Brother Sun' in their midst, adding the stanza, 'Praised be You, my Lord, through those who give pardon for Your love and bear infirmity and tribulation. / Blessed are those who endure in peace.' When the rival parties heard the song, they were so moved that they repented of their mutual hatred, and reconciled.

This was a song, then, that not only reconciled Francis to his fate, but also reconciled people one to another and to their God.

Parchment
containing a
handwritten note
from Francis to
Brother Leo.

Sister Death

F rancis was at San Damiano when he composed 'The Canticle of Brother Sun'. Before he left, he composed another song for the Poor Ladies who had so faithfully cared for him. In the summer of 1225, he also wrote them a letter, encouraging them to continue 'to live and die' in their 'austere and poor' life. There was much weeping as he left for Reiti.

Reiti was the papal courts' home away from Rome, and where some of Italy's best physicians were to be found. Francis, under a papal command, now made his way to their care, though dreading every step. He abhorred being fussed over by Elias and others, even if his health was suffering. Besides, travel was painful. The brothers had to wrap his face in cloth so that sunlight would not penetrate and sear his eyes. Still, his infected eyes wept continually.

Pope Honorius and Cardinal Ugolino warmly welcomed Francis, whose presence in the city created an immediate stir. Merchants broke off business engagements to ask his advice or hear him talk. The ill sought his prayers for healing. Many hangers-on simply wanted to bask in the presence of someone who was clearly headed for sainthood.

To escape such attention, Francis moved to a country church, five kilometres from Reiti. Still, parties of cardinals, bishops and their retainers, and other curious clergy, still sought out the holy celebrity. Finally, Francis retired to a hermitage in the woods of Fonte Colombo, where earlier he had completed his Rule. He underwent further eye treatments, but with no success.

Elias and Ugolino recommended a trip to Siena, where more doctors could be consulted. But one night, soon after he arrived, Francis began vomiting uncontrollably, and

'Listen, poor ones called by the Lord, who have come together from many parts and provinces. Live always in truth, that you may die in obedience. Do not look at the life without, for that of the Spirit is better.'

FRANCIS, 'CANTICLE OF EXHORTATION TO THE POOR LADIES OF SAN DAMIANO', 1225

blood started coming up. Everyone thought that this was the end. Then he recovered. Then he suffered a relapse.

It was clear that Francis's 46-year-old body was slipping away. Today, medical scholars believe that Francis suffered from osteoporosis, fatal malnutrition (probably from excessive fasting), possibly tuberculosis, a peptic or stomach ulcer and the side effects of malaria (contracted in North Africa). His stomach began to swell, as did his legs and feet, due to dropsy, and he could take in no food. Elias rushed him to Assisi, so that Francis could die in his hometown.

Medieval medicine

In addition to the illnesses which plague all ages, medieval people had to deal with scourges that are rarely known today: smallpox, leprosy, St Antony's fire and St Vitus's dance. Such illnesses were the product of overcrowding and unsanitary living conditions, as well as malnutrition.

Most medieval people believed that disease was the result of an imbalance in the four bodily fluids, or humours: choler, phlegm, black bile and blood. Restoring the balance was seen as the path to health. Cauterization, surgery, diet and herbal medicine were all used to restore that balance. But the most popular method was bloodletting – a specific vein was opened to treat a specific disease, and the blood was then analysed for its smell or greasiness.

Later medieval doctors were guided by elaborately illustrated charts, helping them to inspect the patient's urine (for colour, smell and sedimentation). They also used calendars and tables for applying astrological medicine, or manuals depicting herbs and their applications. By the end of the Middle Ages, cadavers were being experimented on to further medical science.

Only the wealthy or well-connected (such as Francis) were able to afford physicians, though some 13th-century Italian cities retained physicians for their citizens. Otherwise, peasants had to depend on local folk healers – and prayer.

The last months

During these last months of his life, Francis became increasingly anxious about his order. He had formally resigned as its head six years earlier, and he had dutifully submitted to the new minister general, Elias (as of 1221). But he became increasingly nervous about the direction which the increasingly large order was taking. The larger the order, the more layers of administration it needed. And, with that, came a pastoral relaxation of the Rule to accommodate the weaknesses of those who had joined, but who had not been inspired by Francis's original vision. Perhaps he sensed how Elias would guide the order after Francis's death, with an authoritarian hand and a more luxurious lifestyle.

For all his symbolic acts of letting go, Francis understandably could not quite let go. In the last weeks and months of his life, he composed a document, a sermon to his brothers, calling them back to his pristine vision. It is called *The Testament*.

This 12th-century medieval manuscript illumination shows patients being treated for haemorrhoids, nasal polyps and cataracts.

This reliquary
holds bones said
to be from the
hand of John the
Baptist.

In the first part, Francis reminisces. He remembers how lepers were 'too bitter for me to see', and how, after showing them mercy, 'what had seemed bitter to me was turned into sweetness of soul and body'. He recalls the early prayer he adapted as he went about churches: 'We adore you, Lord Jesus Christ, in all your church throughout the whole world and we bless you because by your holy cross you have redeemed the world.'

Francis's relics at home

Elias made haste to get Francis to Assisi because he knew his world. It was important that Francis die and be buried in the town he was associated with, so that his hometown could house his relics.

Medieval piety was rooted in the veneration of saints and their *relicta* ('things left behind'). Christians, especially, believed that the barrier between this life and the next could be bridged. They also believed that saints were not dead, any more than was Jesus. Church teachers said that the prayers of saints could be sought from anywhere, but people came to believe that saints were especially present at the saints' shrines – Peter at Rome, James at Compostela, Thomas Becket at Canterbury. At shrines, the saints' bones, or items associated with the saint (such as a part of the sword that slew the martyr), were held in a reliquary. People flocked to such places to say their prayers. They often expected miracles, especially healing, at shrines. At a minimum, they expected to experience some sense of transcendence there, where they believed that a bit of heaven was touching earth.

To be sure, a popular shrine garnered income for local merchants and for the church, but it is too cynical to say this was the only reason for which Assisi officials would want Francis to be buried in his hometown. No doubt civic pride played some role, as well. But, more than anything, the town fathers wanted Francis close because they wanted to be close to heaven.

Then comes an extensive paragraph on his loyalty to his church: 'The Lord gave me, and gives me still, such faith in priests who live according to the rite of the holy Roman Church because of their orders that, were they to persecute me, I would still want to have recourse to them.'

In fact, the order still experienced hostility in parts of Christendom, and it attracted people who were disgusted with the church and who sought a purer path to holiness. For these and other reasons, in less than a century, some later Franciscans found themselves seriously at odds with the hierarchy. Some were even excommunicated as heretics and burned to death. Francis, no doubt, sensed that the seeds of alienation had already been planted. He spends considerable words in *The Testament* to mandate faithfulness to things Catholic: 'We must honour all theologians and those who minister the most holy divine words and respect them as those who minister us spirit and life.'

'Who are these people? They have snatched out of my hands my religion and that of the brothers. If I go to the general chapter, I'll show them what is my will.'

FRANCIS, AFTER A SEVERE ILLNESS LATER IN LIFE, *THE ASSISI COMPILATION* (1244–60)

Then come a variety of reminiscences about the life of poverty, each of which seems to be an indirect admonition to the brothers. He notes that the early brothers 'were content with one tunic, patched inside and out, with a cord and short trousers'. Then Francis adds, 'We desired nothing more.' He remembers, 'I worked with my hands, and I still desire to work; and I earnestly desire all the brothers to give themselves to honest work.'

To be sure, he had given the brothers permission to do other things, such as pursue study, but Francis was having second thoughts, and for good reason. In the next generation, the order would produce men who were known less for their poverty, humility, service or Christ-likeness, and more for their great learning. A few examples are: Alexander of Hales,

Theologian John Duns Scotus, the brilliant Franciscan rival of the Dominican Thomas Aquinas. Portrait by Joos van Gent.

*'Francis saw
many rushing
for positions of
authority.
Despising their
arrogance, he
strove by his
own example to
call them back
from such
sickness.'*

THOMAS OF CELANO,
*THE LIFE OF
ST FRANCIS*, 1228–29

the 'Irrefragible Doctor'; Bonaventure, the 'Seraphic Doctor,'; Roger Bacon, the 'Admirable Doctor'; Ockham, the 'Invincible Doctor'; and Duns Scotus, the famous rival of Thomas Aquinas.

Shifting gears, Francis then moves into direct admonitions: 'Let the brothers be careful not to receive in any way churches or poor dwellings or anything built for them unless they are according to the holy poverty we have promised in the Rule.' In fact, the order had gradually begun accepting some churches and residences, and Francis had tacitly agreed to these exceptions. But, again, he was questioning his former flexibility.

Furthermore, says Francis, 'I strictly command all the brothers through obedience, where they may be, not to dare to ask any letter from the Roman Curia... whether for a church or another place or under the pretext of preaching or the persecution of their bodies.' Again, this is a matter which Francis had, through his silence, let slide.

He also tells the brothers to recite the daily Office according to the Rule. And any who do not are to be brought before the nearest custodian who, in turn, will 'keep him securely day and night as a man in chains' and 'personally deliver him into the hands of his minister'. The minister, in turn, 'would guard him as a prisoner' until he can be handed over to the Protector of the Order.

Though Francis says that he is not writing 'another Rule', he does say that the brothers are 'bound through obedience not to add to or take away from these words'. Then he adds, 'And let them always have this writing with them together with the Rule'. In other words, this document was the key to interpreting the Rule. 'I strictly command all my cleric and lay brothers, through obedience,' he says, 'not to place any gloss upon the Rule or upon these words, saying, "They should be understood in this way."'

It is clear that Francis felt that the order was softening, that its vision was fuzzy, and that the brothers were settling into a reasonable, ordered life of moderate devotion.

Francis, no doubt, also realized that he himself was being slighted. His pleas are punctuated by the repeated phrase 'through obedience', a desperate attempt to bring the brothers back into conformity by the force of his personality. As it turned out, this was an exercise in futility. The order simply could not sustain his pure vision without his saintly presence. Mere mortals were simply incapable of living day by day with the intensity that his ideals demanded.

Ultimately, Francis recognized the futility of his *Testament* because, during this same period, he told a story that captured the irony of his rejection by his order. The story illustrates Francis's longing for utter self-denial which, paradoxically, led Francis to experience a type of joy that few people have known. It is in the very rejection of his ideals that his personal aspirations were fulfilled. A 14th-century manuscript contains a condensed version of a longer version recorded in *The Little Flowers of St Francis*:

One day at Saint Mary [of the Angels], Francis called Brother Leo and said, 'Brother Leo, write this down.'

He answered, 'I'm ready.'

'Write what true joy is,' he said. 'A messenger comes and says that all the masters of theology in Paris have joined the order – write: that is not true joy. Or all the prelates beyond the mountains – archbishops and bishops, or the king of France and the king of England – write: that is not true joy. Or that my friars have gone to the unbelievers and have converted all of them to the faith; or that I have so much grace from God that I heal the sick and I perform many miracles. I tell you all that true joy is not all those things.'

'But what is true joy?'

'I am returning from Perugia, and I am coming here at night, in the dark. It is wintertime and wet and muddy and so cold that icicles form at the edges of my habit and keep striking my legs, and blood flows from such wounds. And I come to the gate, all covered with mud and cold and ice, and after I have knocked and called for a long time, a friar comes and asks, "Who are you?"

A highly stylized
and symbolic
depiction of
Francis's death
and ascension, in
which St Francis
is attended by
angels on his
way to heaven,
while below, the
brothers surround
his earthly body.
*Death of
St Francis* by
Giotto di
Bondone.

'I answer, "Brother Francis."

'And he says, "Go away. This is not a decent time to be going about. You can't come in."

'And when I insist again, he replies, "Go away. You are a simple and uneducated fellow. From now on, don't stay with us any more. We are so many and so important that we don't need you."

'But I stand at the gate and say, "For the love of God, let me come in tonight."

'And he answers, "I won't. Go to the Crosier's Place [lepers' hospital] and ask there."

'I tell you that if I kept patience and was not upset – that is true joy and true virtue and salvation of the soul.'

So, despite the fact that his order seemed to be saying, 'We don't need you,' Francis was dying in joy. At the end, in fact, it was this very joy that further scandalized his brothers.

He had been brought to the bishop's palace in Assisi in late summer 1226 and, when he experienced violent attacks of pain, he asked the brothers to sing to him 'The Canticle of Brother Sun', both night and day. When Elias, among others, heard about this, he told Francis that it was unseemly for him to be rejoicing like this. People were talking. He scolded Francis: a saint, which the people considered him to be, should be preparing for his death in a more solemn and holy fashion.

Francis patiently asked him to indulge him in this, 'For by the grace and assistance of the Holy Spirit, I am so united and conjoined to my Lord that by his mercy I may rightly rejoice in him, the Most High.'

Even that was not enough for Francis; it was at this time that he added the stanza about death to his 'Canticle':

Praised be you, my Lord, through our Sister Bodily Death,
  from whom no living man can escape
Woe to those who die in mortal sin.
Blessed are those whom death will find in Your most holy will,
  for the second death shall do them no harm.

When Francis felt that death was imminent, he asked to
be carried to the Portiuncula. Halfway down the slope
from Assisi, he told his bearers to stop so that he could
bless his hometown. He was finally put down in a hut
a few metres from the chapel of St Mary of the Angels.
In honour of Lady Poverty, he asked to be placed on the
ground naked but, finally, at the insistence of the brothers,

Clare adores the
stigmata of
Francis on his
deathbed.
*St Clare Grieving
Over the Body of
St Francis* by
Giotto di
Bondone.

he agreed to return to his bed. He absolved and blessed the brothers, listened to readings from the Gospel of John and had the brothers sing his 'Canticle' again.

Then, on 3 October, as Thomas of Celano describes it, 'The most holy soul was released from the flesh, and it was absorbed into the abyss of light, his body fell asleep in the Lord.'

One brother thought that he saw the soul of Francis rise to heaven, 'like a star but as big as the moon, with the brilliance of the sun, and carried up upon a small white cloud'. Others later said that a great flock of birds descended on the hut, circling and singing with 'unusual joy'.

'Naked he lingered before the bishop at the beginning of his conversion; and for this reason, at the end of his life, he wanted to leave this world naked.'

BONAVENTURE, *THE MAJOR LEGEND OF ST FRANCIS*, 1260–63

C H A P T E R   1 3

The Modern Medieval Man

Previous pages:
The Basilica San
Francesco in
Assisi – an ironic
way to honour
the 'little poor
man'.

T he following spring, Francis's longtime mentor, Cardinal Ugolino, became Pope Gregory IX. As one of his first acts, he pushed Francis's canonization through the necessary bureaucratic hoops, so that Francis was made an official saint

Medieval burial

Before Christianity took root in Europe, a variety of burial customs was practised. The Jutes, like the Romans before them, buried their remains. The Angles, Saxons and Scandinavians cremated the body, After the arrival of Christianity, cremation was abandoned in favour of burial, so that the dead might have bodies to meet the Lord on Judgment Day. Furthermore, no longer were the deceased buried with grave goods, such as weapons, jewellery or coins, since none of this was thought to be necessary in the afterlife.

The rich were the only class which could afford elaborately carved stone coffins but, by the end of the Middle Ages, wooden coffins had become the norm for all classes.

Francis's death presented some special difficulties. Everyone knew that Francis was headed for sainthood. The temptation to raid his tomb and steal his bones as relics would be almost irresistible. So Elias and Gregory went to great lengths to bury his tomb deep within the Basilica San Franceso – under a slab of granite, gravel, and 10 welded bands of iron, an 86-kilogram grill and, finally, a 91-kilogram rock. The plan worked. The coffin was not discovered and unearthed until the beginning of the 19th century.

in July 1228 – less than two years after his death. In
May 1230, Francis's remains were moved from the San
Giorgio Church to a new basilica: Basilica San Francesco
(the Church of St Francis), built under the direction of
Brother Elias.

Elias had been replaced as the order's head in 1227,
but Gregory gave him the job of building an appropriate
basilica in Francis's honour. To many followers, the
grand, ornate building that emerged was anything but
appropriate. Many brothers were shocked, not only at
the imposing structure, but at how Elias had badgered
provincials to raise money to build it. It was, they felt,
an utter contradiction of everything Francis stood for.

On the other hand, Gregory and Elias were not alone

Medieval burial
scene from a
16th-century
French
manuscript.

in admiring the basilica. Many other brothers thought
it a shrine worthy of their holy founder. Nor were they
scandalized, as some were, when Gregory named it (and
not the humble St Mary's) as the 'head and mother' of
the order.

These developments only widened a split in the order

The towering
grandeur of
Chartres
Cathedral.

that Francis saw coming. His *Testament* was an attempt to get all the brothers to commit themselves again to strict poverty. Now the new minister general, John Parenti, tried to take up the dying Francis's dying cause. He appealed to Gregory to make *The Testament* binding on the order.

The medieval cathedral

Francis's era saw the rise of Gothic architecture and the beginning of many of Europe's grandest architectural projects. The Basilica San Francesco in Assisi was not a grand project such as Chartres or Rouen, but it was inspired by cathedrals such as these.

The scale of these building projects pushed medieval architecture to its limits. Massive amounts of material were required. Ely Cathedral in England took more than 363,000 kilograms of wood and stone to finish. Whole forests were felled in France to complete some projects. Eighteen-metre-long beams were imported from Scandinavia. Stone for the Norwich Cathedral was shipped from 483 kilometres away (making the cost of shipping twice the price of the stone itself).

New machinery had to be constructed. To lift heavy carved stones high up a cathedral roof, workers used winches, windlasses and a 'great wheel' – a wooden wheel which was large enough for one or two men to stand inside.

The amount of detailed work seemed unending. Although some stained-glass windows were as high as 18 metres, they still had to be made up of pieces no larger than 20 centimetres wide or high. Cathedrals included dozens, if not hundreds, of sculptures – Chartres Cathedral today has more than 2,000.

And then there was the patience required; some cathedrals took more than 100 years to build, and some bishops spent their entire tenure holding church services in the middle of a huge construction site. Yet, despite the architectural and financial challenges, during one 400-year period, Europe saw the construction of some 500 cathedrals.

*'I have done
what is mine to
do; may Christ
teach you what
you are to do.'*

FRANCIS TO HIS
BROTHERS ON HIS
DEATHBED

*Opposite page:
The Canonization
of St Francis.*
Altar panel
attributed to
Bonaventura
Berlinghieri in the
Bardi chapel,
Santa Croce,
Florence.

*'Today we
take it for
granted that if
you are deeply
committed
to the gospel,
you will go into
the world to
serve. That
assumption is
due in large
measure to
Francis's
ministry.'*

CONRAD
HAWKINS OFM,
ST BONAVENTURE
UNIVERSITY,
NEW YORK,
CHRISTIAN HISTORY
MAGAZINE, 1994

Gregory saw no future in that. He believed that Francis's radical vision could not be sustained, and that strict adherence to *The Testament* would undermine the future growth and stability of the order. So he announced that the more moderate Rule of 1223 would be the standard. Furthermore, he said, money could now be held on behalf of the order, and friars were to be allowed books and other personal effects. They would also be permitted to use and live in large and permanent buildings.

Franciscan divisions

The subsequent history of the order is both complex and bitter. The rift between the champions of strict poverty – soon called the 'Spirituals' – and the moderates widened. By 1317, the Spirituals had become such an irritant to church authorities that they were excommunicated as heretics. Some were arrested and burned at the stake.

This did not solve the Franciscan dilemma: how were ordinary mortals to sustain an order founded on the ideals of a saintly personality? In the 1330s, some friars south of Assisi again took up a 'stricter observance' of the Rule. Avoiding some of the extremist rhetoric of the Spirituals, they managed to gain papal recognition for their efforts in 1415. In 1443, they were given their own minister general and, in 1517, they were separated from the main Franciscan body (known as the 'Conventuals'), and are today known as 'Observants'.

But, by 1525, some Observants began to question the purity of their order, and Matteo da Basci led a movement to live by Francis's Rule more literally. In 1529, the pope permitted them also to become an independent order, the Capuchins, an order that today emphasizes contemplative prayer.

Today, these three orders combined make up the largest order in the Roman Catholic Church. Added to this are the Order of St Clare, the Episcopalian

Franciscan Orders and the Order of secular Franciscans in many denominations. The overall numbers are not overly impressive, totalling in the tens of thousands – some Pentecostal congregations in Korea and Brazil are larger. But numbers are not everything. Francis continues to have an influence beyond the devotion of his formal adherents.

Unfortunately, this influence is narrow in scope. For the larger world, Francis has become a statue to be placed in gardens or, more seriously, the patron saint of two modern movements – those of peace and ecology. Very few people today show much interest in Francis's deep personal faith, his call to strict poverty or his absolute devotion to the Roman Catholic Church. In fact, many Catholics in the peace and ecology movements, who regularly name Francis as their champion, pride themselves in rebelling against the established church, showing nothing but disdain for the hierarchy – a fact which their patron saint would deplore.

'Beyond the romantic clichés about St Francis, one discovers a person who, for all of his transparent attractiveness, is complex to the point of enigma.'

LAWRENCE S. CUNNINGHAM, *ST FRANCIS OF ASSISI*, 1981

This selective admiration is reinforced by the popularity of two poems, which people believe best summarize Francis's life and thought. Unfortunately, in both instances, the real Francis is misrepresented.

One is his 'Canticle of Brother Sun'. In this case, modern readers show a remarkable ability to skip over the opening stanza:

Most High, all-powerful, good Lord,
   yours are the praises, the glory, the honour, and all
      blessing.

Man in the Street Pays Homage to St Francis by Giotto di Bondone.

To you alone, Most High, do they belong,
*   and no man is worthy to mention your name.*

And they remain deaf to the repeated references to God throughout. In other words, the poem in their minds is an ode to the wonders of nature. Francis becomes, for them, merely a troubadour of the environment. This is despite the poem's clear intention to glorify not creation, but the Creator.

The other poem that has gained popularity since the 20th century goes like this:

Lord, make me an instrument of your peace.
Where there is hatred, let me sow love;
*   where there is injury, pardon;*
where there is doubt, faith;
*   where there is despair, hope;*
where there is darkness, light;
*   where there is sadness, joy.*

O Divine Master, grant that I may not so much seek to be
*   consoled as to console;*
*   to be understood as to understand;*
to be loved as to love;
*   for it is in giving that we receive;*
it is in pardoning that we are pardoned;
*   it is in dying that we are born again to eternal life.*

Most readers assume that these words come from Francis himself. Not quite. Though he expressed many of these sentiments in his life, he never did so in this form. As far as we can tell, it was first composed at a Catholic eucharistic congress that met in Chicago, Illinois, in 1925. To be sure, it represents one theme of Francis's life and teachings – but only one.

Thus we come to the unhappy conclusion that the

Francis who is remembered and adored today is not the Francis who walked the Umbrian roads in the 13th century. But this is not surprising. The real Francis makes every age a tad uncomfortable. The Francis who calls us to peace and respect for creation – causes we readily sign up for – is the same Francis who challenges our age, as he did his own age, by speaking and living against our most vexing sins.

In a secular age, when talk of God is awkward or rigidly privatized, stands the deeply pious Francis, whose God-intoxication drove everything he did. In a materialistic world, where the meaning and measure of life is counted by the things we buy and the experiences we enjoy, the barefoot, raggedly robed Francis calls us to simplicity and poverty. In cultures drowning in rampant individualism, in which we baulk at submitting to anything outside the self, Francis tells us to abandon our lives in complete obedience to something bigger than ourselves.

In short, Francis would instil in us, as he tried to instil in his contemporaries, profound gratitude and humility – towards God, our world and even the flawed institutions that have nurtured us. In the end, although our modern world wishes to

discard so much of Francis into the rubbish bin of
history, it is the medieval Francis who shows the modern
world a better way.

Opposite page:
This portrait is
considered by
many to be the
most accurate of
Francis. From
Maestà by
Giovanni
Cimabue, Basilica
San Francesco,
Assisi.

Chronology

Summer or autumn 1181: Giovanni di Pietro di Bernardone is born and baptized in Assisi; the child is renamed Francesco by his father.

1190: Francis attends the parish school at San Giorgio.

1193: Chiara di Favarone (Clare) is born to a noble Assisi family.

1199–1200: Civil war in Assisi; destruction of feudal nobles' castles. Some Assisi families (including Clare's) move to Perugia.

November 1202: War between Perugia and Assisi; Assisi defeated at the Battle of Collestrada. Francis spends a year in prison in Perugia, until ransomed by his father.

1204: Francis is slowly healed of the illness contracted in prison.

Spring 1205: Francis sets out for war in Apulia but returns the next day after receiving a vision in Spoleto. This is the beginning of his gradual conversion.

Autumn to winter 1205: Francis receives the message of the crucifix of San Damiano. He is mocked by fellow Assisians. He prays and meditates in countryside caves.

January or February 1206: Francis's conflict with his father ends with a trial before Bishop Guido.

Spring 1206: Francis nurses leprosy victims in Gubbio. From summer through winter, he repairs San Damiano, San Pietro and the Portiuncula.

24 February 1208: Francis hears the Gospel of St Mathias Mass. He changes from hermit's habit to that of barefoot preacher; he begins to preach.

Spring 1208: Bernard, Peter Cantanii and Giles join Francis at the Portiuncula; they embark on their first mission. By the end of the year, four more join the order.

Early 1209: When the group returns from another mission, another four recruits join them, bringing the total to 12 (including Francis).

Spring 1209: Francis writes a brief Rule and obtains informal approval for his order from Pope Innocent III. On their return, the brothers stay briefly Rivo Torto.

1209/10: The friars move to the Portiuncula.

Night of 18–19 March 1212 (Palm Sunday): Francis receives Clare at the Portiuncula; she moves to San Damiano in May.

1213: Francis receives the gift of Mount Verna, which he uses as a hermitage.

1213–14 or 1214–15: Francis travels to Spain and back.

November 1215: Francis is in Rome for the Fourth Lateran Council. He meets Dominic.

Summer 1216: Honorius III is elected pope upon Innocent III's death. The new pope gives Francis the Portiuncula Indulgence.

5 May 1217: Five thousand brothers convene at the Pentecost general chapter at the Portiuncula. The first Franciscan missions take place in Germany, Tunis and Syria.

1219: After the general chapter, another overseas mission is inaugurated. Francis sails from Ancona for Acre and Damietta. He crosses crusader battle lines to preach to the Muslim sultan.

1220: The first Franciscan martyrs are killed, in Morocco. Francis goes to Acre and Holy Land. Cardinal Hugolin appointed Protector of the Order

1220: Francis resigns as head of his order. He appoints Peter Cantanii as vicar.

1221: Elias becomes vicar after Peter Cantanii's death. The Rule of the Third Order is approved by Honorius III.

1221–22: Francis goes on a preaching tour in southern Italy.

15 August 1222: Francis preaches in Bologna.

Early 1223: Francis composes the Second Rule. The Rule is discussed at the June general chapter. Pope Honorius III approves it in November.

24–25 December 1223: Francis celebrates the Christmas crèche Midnight Mass at Greccio.

15 August–29 September 1224: Francis fasts at La Verna and receives the stigmata.

December 1224–February 1225: A weakened Francis rides a donkey to make a preaching tour in Umbria and the Marches.

Early 1225: Nearly blind from an eye problem, Francis is cared for by Clare at San Damiano. Francis composes 'The Canticle of Brother Sun'. He reconciles the feuding bishop and *podesta* of Assisi.

Summer 1225 to summer 1226: Francis travels. He receives various treatments for his various illnesses, to no avail.

September 1226: Knowing his death is imminent, Francis insists on being carried to the Portiuncula. He dies on 3 October and is buried the next day at San Giorgio Church.

19 March 1227: His friend Hugolin becomes Pope Gregory IX.

16 July 1228: Gregory IX canonizes St Francis.

25 May 1230: Francis's remains are moved to his new basilica, Basilica San Francesco in Assisi.

(Adapted from Omer Englebert, *St Francis of Assisi: A Biography*, Franciscan Herald Press, 1965, pp. 393–96, and Joanne Schatzlein, 'Francis of Assisi 1181–1226: The Christian History Timeline' in *Christian History*, Issue 21, No. 2, spring 1994, pp. 26–27.)

Suggestions for Further Reading

Primary sources

Regis J. Armstrong, J.A. Wayne Hellmann and William Short (eds), *Francis of Assisi: Early Documents*, Volume 1, *The Saint*, New York: New City, 1999.

Regis J. Armstrong, J.A. Wayne Hellmann and William Short (eds), *Francis of Assisi: Early Documents*, Volume 2, *The Founder*, New York: New City, 2000.

Regis J. Armstrong and Ignatius Brady (eds and trs), *Francis and Clare: The Complete Works*, New York: Paulist Press, 1982.

Martin Habig, *St Francis of Assisi, Writings and Early Biographies: English Omnibus of the Sources for the Life of St Francis*, Quincey, Illinois: Franciscan Press, 1991.

Biographies

Omer Englebert, *St Francis of Assisi: A Biography*, Chicago: Franciscan Herald Press, 1965.

Arnaldo Fortini, *Francis of Assisi*, tr. Helen Moak, New York: Crossroad, 1992.

Julian Green, *God's Fool: The Life and Times of Francis of Assisi*, San Francisco: Harper, 1985.

Adrian House, *Francis of Assisi: A Revolutionary Life*, Mahwah, New Jersey: Hidden Spring, 2000, 2001.

Johannes Jörgensen, *St Francis of Assisi: A Biography*, tr. T. O'Conor Sloan, New York: Doubleday, 1955 (1912).

Michael Robson, *St Francis of Assisi: The Legend and the Life*, London: Geoffrey Chapman, 1997.

Paul Sabatier, *Life of St Francis of Assisi*, tr. Louise Seymour Houghton, New York: Scribners, 1905.

Reflective interpretations of Francis

G.K. Chesterton, *St Francis of Assisi*, New York: Doubleday, 1924, 1957.

Nikos Kazantzakis, *St Francis: A Novel*, New York: Simon and Schuster, 1962.

Roy M. Gasnick (ed.), *The Francis Book: 800 Years with the Saint from Assisi*, New York: Macmillan, 1980.

Valerie Martin, *Salvation: Scenes from the Life of St Francis*, New York: Knopf, 2001.

Gerard Thomas Straub, *The Sun and Moon Over Assisi: A Personal Encounter with Francis and Clare*, New York: Saint Anthony Messenger Press, 2000.

Middle Ages, miscellany

Adrian H. Bredero, *Christendom and Christianity in the Middle Ages*, Grand Rapids, Michigan: Eerdmans, 1986, 1984.

Christopher Dawson, *Religion and the Rise of Western Culture*, New York: Doubleday, 1957.

Frances Gies, *The Knight in History*, San Francisco: Harper & Row, 1984.

J.R.H. Moorman, *A History of the Franciscan Order from its Origins to the Year 1517*, Oxford: Clarendon Press, 1968.

R.W. Southern, *Western Society and Church in the Middle Ages*, London: Penguin, 1993.

André Vauchez, *The Laity in the Middle Ages: Religious Beliefs and Devotional Practices*, ed. and tr. Daniel E. Bornstein, South Bend, Indiana: Notre Dame, 1993.

Index

Picture and Text Acknowledgments

Pictures

Picture research by Zooid Pictures Limited.

AKG London: pp. 1 (S. Domingie), 4 (Stefan Diller), 6–7 (Schütze/Rodemann), 16–17 (British Library), 21, 22–23 (British Library), 29 (British Library), 46 (Stefan Diller), 49 (Stefan Diller), 60, 62–63, 72–73 (Erich Lessing), 76 (Chantilly, Musée Condé), 86–87, 88 (Stefan Diller), 109 (Stefan Diller), 116 (S. Domingie), 122–23 (VISIOARS), 127 (Stefan Diller), 132 (Stefan Diller), 138 (Erich Lessing), 152, 157, 163 (British Library), 172–73 (Stefan Diller), 175, 179 (Stefan Diller), 182.

Bridgeman Art Library: pp. 98–99 (British Library).

Corbis UK Ltd: pp. 2 (Elio Ciol), 12 (Gustavo Tomsich), 18 (Austrian Archives), 26 (National Gallery Collection; by kind permission of the Trustees of the National Gallery, London), 34 (Gianni Dagli Orti), 36–37 (Elio Ciol), 42–43 (Elio Ciol), 55 (Archivo Iconografico, S.A.), 58 (Jay Syverson), 74–75 (Mark L. Stephenson), 80–81 (Elio Ciol), 82 (Vanni Archive), 90–91 (Archivo Iconografico, S.A.), 92–93 (Elio Ciol), 104 (Elio Ciol), 112 (Gianni Dagli Orti), 136 (Archivo Iconografico, S.A.), 145 (Arte & Immagini SRL), 148–49 (Elio Ciol), 154 (National Gallery Collection; by kind permission of the Trustees of the National Gallery, London), 165 (Gianni Dagli Orti), 168–69 (Elio Ciol), 170 (Elio Ciol), 176–77 (Craig Aurness), 180 (Elio Ciol).

Mary Evans Picture Library: p. 53.

Scala: pp. 38, 56, 160.

Werner Forman Archive: p. 164.

Derek West: maps on pp. 10–11, 44–45, 64.

Text

Except for page 157, the scripture quotations contained herein are from The New Revised Standard Version of the Bible, Anglicized Edition, copyright © 1989, 1995 by the Division of Christian Education of the National Council of the Churches of Christ in the United States of America, and are used by permission. All rights reserved.

Extract on page 157 taken from the New Jerusalem Bible, published and copyright © 1985 by Darton, Longman and Todd Ltd and les Editions du Cerf, and by Doubleday, a division of Bantam Doubleday Dell Publishing Group, Inc. Used by permission of Darton, Longman and Todd Ltd, and Doubleday, a division of Random House, Inc.

Excerpts on pages 100–101 (poem from the end of the Rule of St Francis) and pages 158–60 ('The Canticle of Brother Sun') from *Francis and Clare: The Complete Works*, tr. Regis Armstrong and Ignatius Brady, copyright © 1982. Used with permisson of Paulist Press. Available at bookstores or www.paulistpress.com or 1-800-218-1903.

Lion Publishing

Commissioning editor: Morag Reeve

Project editor: Jenni Dutton

Insides designer: Nicholas Rous

Jacket designer: Jonathan Roberts

Production controller: Charles Wallis